Karen Bale

Media Representations of Female Body Images in Women's Magazines

Karen Bale

Media Representations of Female Body Images in Women's Magazines

A Content Analysis of Media Trends

VDM Verlag Dr. Müller

Impressum/Imprint (nur für Deutschland/ only for Germany)

Bibliografische Information der Deutschen Nationalbibliothek: Die Deutsche Nationalbibliothek verzeichnet diese Publikation in der Deutschen Nationalbibliografie; detaillierte bibliografische Daten sind im Internet über http://dnb.d-nb.de abrufbar.

Alle in diesem Buch genannten Marken und Produktnamen unterliegen warenzeichen-, marken- oder patentrechtlichem Schutz bzw. sind Warenzeichen oder eingetragene Warenzeichen der jeweiligen Inhaber. Die Wiedergabe von Marken, Produktnamen, Gebrauchsnamen, Handelsnamen, Warenbezeichnungen u.s.w. in diesem Werk berechtigt auch ohne besondere Kennzeichnung nicht zu der Annahme, dass solche Namen im Sinne der Warenzeichen- und Markenschutzgesetzgebung als frei zu betrachten wären und daher von jedermann benutzt werden dürften.

Coverbild: www.purestockx.com

Verlag: VDM Verlag Dr. Müller Aktiengesellschaft & Co. KG
Dudweiler Landstr. 99, 66123 Saarbrücken, Deutschland
Telefon +49 681 9100-698, Telefax +49 681 9100-988, Email: info@vdm-verlag.de
Zugl.: Stillwater, Oklahoma State University, Diss., 2006

Herstellung in Deutschland:
Schaltungsdienst Lange o.H.G., Berlin
Books on Demand GmbH, Norderstedt
Reha GmbH, Saarbrücken
Amazon Distribution GmbH, Leipzig
ISBN: 978-3-639-09384-1

Imprint (only for USA, GB)

Bibliographic information published by the Deutsche Nationalbibliothek: The Deutsche Nationalbibliothek lists this publication in the Deutsche Nationalbibliografie; detailed bibliographic data are available in the Internet at http://dnb.d-nb.de.

Any brand names and product names mentioned in this book are subject to trademark, brand or patent protection and are trademarks or registered trademarks of their respective holders. The use of brand names, product names, common names, trade names, product descriptions etc. even without a particular marking in this works is in no way to be construed to mean that such names may be regarded as unrestricted in respect of trademark and brand protection legislation and could thus be used by anyone.

Cover image: www.purestockx.com

Publisher:
VDM Verlag Dr. Müller Aktiengesellschaft & Co. KG
Dudweiler Landstr. 99, 66123 Saarbrücken, Germany
Phone +49 681 9100-698, Fax +49 681 9100-988, Email: info@vdm-publishing.com
Copyright © 2008 VDM Verlag Dr. Müller Aktiengesellschaft & Co. KG and licensors
All rights reserved. Saarbrücken 2008

Printed in the U.S.A.
Printed in the U.K. by (see last page)
ISBN: 978-3-639-09384-1

TABLE OF CONTENTS

CHAPTER I

INTRODUCTION

Researchers have discovered the need to achieve physical attractiveness puts substantial pressures on some females. Bennett (2003) found that advertisements in women's magazines can directly affect some females' perceptions of their bodies.

According to Body Image and Advertising (2000), the idealized female body images presented by the media represent standards of femininity that are unrealistic for most women to attain. These media images create frustration and disappointment for some women in Western cultures because they perpetuate unattainable, ideal body standards that can lead to unhealthy eating behaviors.

Murray, Touyz, and Beumont (1996), University of Western Sydney and Touyz Department of Medical Psychology at Westmead Hospital, note that sociocultural factors such as the media continually promote particular body standards for women. During a two-year period, these researchers interviewed eating disorder patients to investigate the role of the media in influencing eating disorder symptomatology. Their findings suggested that sociocultural factors such as the media support the attainment of a thin body shape for women.

Body Image and Advertising (2000) concurs that prevalent marketing strategies presented in advertisements enhance product consumption by promoting unrealistic ideals of body image in women. It further states that continuous exposure to these advertisements can have a negative effect on women's perceptions of their bodies and their evaluations of their physical attractiveness. Mass media such as magazines promote these idealized body images and produce insecurities and body dissatisfaction (Body Image and Advertising, 2000; Stice & Shaw, 1994; U.S. Department of Health and Human Service's Office on Women's Health, 2000).

Dittrich (2004), About-Face director, attempts to develop positive self-images in females through media education, outreach, and activism. Dittrich supports the suggestion that the media have an adverse effect on women's perceptions of their bodies. She notes that the media perpetuate the perception in Western cultures that thinness is a means to attaining social acceptance, happiness, love, and personal and business achievements. According to Dittrich, unrealistic media images of thinness also present ideals that appear to be achievable to the average woman, and these images promote the misconception that the thin female body size represents the standard body weight that women should try to emulate.

In a research study on magazine viewing (Stice, Spangler, and Agras, 2001), 219 female participants were randomly assigned to two groups. One group received subscriptions to fashion magazines for a period of 15 months. The other group did not receive the magazines over the same time period. The researchers concluded "that exposure to thin-ideal images" may have long-term effects on young women (p. 1). These researchers also noted that magazine consumption prompted an increase in women's body dissatisfaction and their desires to be thin.

Tiggemann and Pickering's (1996) study supports the findings of Stice, Spangler, et al. (2001) and suggests when women internalize images of thin female body images they can exhibit negative emotional responses and harmful behaviors. Tiggemann and Pickering (1996) administered questionnaires to 94 women to discover the effects television viewing had on body dissatisfaction and the desire to be thin. The study's findings support a societal link between body dissatisfaction and the types of television programs that are viewed by women. The researchers noted that viewing soaps or serials, music videos, or movies portraying women in stereotypical roles had a negative influence on women's body images.

In 2002, the National Eating Disorders Association (NEDA) reported that 5 million to 10 million women in the United States had developed eating disorder conditions. NEDA also related that $40 billion was spent annually in the United States on diet-related products. Furthermore, NEDA estimated that 40 percent to 50 percent of U.S. females are dissatisfied with their weight and are currently trying to lose weight.

Dittrich (2004) posits that body dissatisfaction and the fear of gaining weight are prevalent emotions in U.S. society, and these emotions prompt some women to pursue the thin ideal body standards that are presented in the media by employing self-destructive behaviors. Dittrich states that about 90 percent to 95 percent of the reported cases of the two most common eating disorders (anorexia and bulimia) occur in women.

Bierma (2003), a health and medical research author, supports the conclusions presented by Dittrich positing that women's dissatisfaction with their bodies poses a cultural problem. One of the societal causes of this cultural concern is the media and the ultra-thin standards the media portray as the ideal, feminine body image. These images are presented to females during the entirety of their lifetimes. This continuous exposure to unrealistic, female body ideals can promote body dissatisfaction, which can contribute to depression, and ultimately, eating disorders (Bierma, 2003; U.S. Department of Health and Human Service's Office on Women's Health, 2000).

According to Mazur (1986), the cultural standard for the ideal female body image is continually changing. Garner, Garfinkel, Schwartz, and Thompson's (1980) findings suggest that there has been a societal trend toward a thinner standard for female body images.

In 1950, Marilyn Monroe was considered "the standard of voluptuous beauty" (Sheehan, 2004, p. 97). Monroe was a major media icon and her images were published in print media such as *Playboy, Family Circle, Yank Magazine, Colliers Magazine, LIFE,* and *Vogue* (Marilyn Monroe.com, 2006). According to a newspaper report by Helser (2004), Monroe was considered to be a size 12 during the 1950s. However, Helser notes that her interviews with a vintage clothing

4

expert and a representative of the Art Institute of Phoenix show that "vanity sizing" practices have changed standard clothing size equivalencies over the past 55 years. What was considered to be a size 12 in the 1950s would have been considered to be a size 6 in 2004. Although Monroe has been referenced as a size 12 by some researchers using today's standards of clothing sizes, according to her official Web site, Marilyn Monroe.com (2006), Monroe was 5 ft 51/2 in tall and her weight varied between 115 lbs and 120 lbs. Her Web site also notes that her dressmaker claimed that her measurements were 35-22-35. Although Monroe may not have weighed as much as some researchers have suggested, Garner, Garfinkel, Schwartz et al. research show that the societal standard for female body image has continued to decrease since 1959.

By the 1960s, there had been a British invasion of the United States by not only the Beatles but also the miniskirt. Models appearing in miniskirts had slender hips and slim legs (Mazur, 1986).

Dixon, Kary, and Maccarone (1999) note that another British influence had an effect on U.S. women's perceptions of the ideal female body in the 1960s - the fashion model Twiggy. Twiggy was 5 ft 7 in tall and weighed 91 lbs. Sheehan (2004) suggests that Twiggy was influential in changing "the standard of beauty" in the United States (p. 97). Dixon et al. (1999) concur that Twiggy established a new standard for the average size of the fashion model in the United States.

According to Silverstein, Perdue, Peterson, and Kelly (1986), the standard for the ideal female body image continued to become slimmer and less shapely during the 1970s. Garner, Garfinkel, Schwarz et al. (1980) suggested in their study of *Playboy* centerfolds and Miss America Pageant contestants, which spanned 1959 through 1978, there was an apparent trend toward continued thinness of *Playboy* models and of Miss America contestants. However, Dixon et al. (1999) and Guillen and Barr (1994) noted that although models continued to become thinner in the 1970s, another trend was emerging in the modeling field; a toned and fit appearance was being endorsed. Therefore, the ideal female body was represented as not only thin but also athletic.

According to Dixon et al. (1999), the focus on the thin, fit body continued to be an important perceptual aspect of the feminine physique in the 1980s. The researchers note the popularity of volumes such as Jane Fonda's *Workout Book* and Susie Orbach's *Fat is a Feminist Issue* were examples of the perceived importance that was placed on fitness during the 1980s as well as the association that existed between being fit and achieving societal success.

Although a fit, toned body type was in vogue, the societal standard for the ideal female body size was continuing to become thinner (Myers & Biocca, 1992). Dixon et al. (1999) noted that during the 1980s the weight of the average model had fallen to 23 percent less than the weight of the average American woman.

Furthermore, during the 1980s, public consciousness of the mental disorder anorexia nervosa was raised, and it became a significant societal concern. This awareness was mainly facilitated by the death of singer Karen Carpenter who suffered from anorexia nervosa and died of cardiac arrest in 1983 (RichardandKarenCarpenter.com, 2006).

In 1990, Wiseman, Gray, Mosimann, and Ahrens (1992) extended the 1959 through 1978 Miss America and *Playboy* centerfold study originally conducted by Garner, Garfinkel, Schwarz et al. (1980). Wiseman et al. (1992) conducted a content analysis of *Playboy* centerfolds from 1979 through 1988 and the Miss America contestants from 1979 through 1985. The researchers noted that the Miss America contestants continued to decrease in body size during 1979 through 1985. The study further showed that *Playboy* centerfolds remained thin during 1979 through 1988. In another study by Turner, Hamilton, Jacobs, Angood, and Dwyer (1997), results suggested media content (in the 1991 women's magazines used in their study) included body images that appeared to influence women to want to weigh less.

By 2000, Brumberg (2000) noted that "a sizeable number of our young women -- poor and privileged alike -- regard their body as the best vehicle for making a statement about their identity and personal dreams" (p. 267). Lightstone (2000) suggested that a woman's thin appearance has become an integral part of the competitive processes that lead to attaining power and public positions. She noted that anorexia and bulimia were prevalent in women seeking positions of success. Furthermore, Harrison and Cantor (1997) noted, "Changes in eating disorder epidemiology over the past 30 years appear to mirror changes in mass media representations of women throughout the same time span" (p. 2).

The U.S. Department of Health and Human Service's Office on Women's Health (2000) concurred in its "February 2000 Information Sheet" that eating disorder related illnesses in U.S. women have doubled during the last three decades. The "February 2000 Information Sheet" estimates that as many as 5 million women are affected by an eating disorder.

The symptoms and behaviors of eating disorders that sometimes develop in females include: heart disease and blood pressure abnormalities, cessation of menstrual periods, bone density issues, fainting and fatigue, hair and skin problems, dehydration, kidney failure, abnormalities of the esophagus and bowels, tooth decay, gallbladder disease, and high cholesterol (NEDA, 2002; U.S. Department of Health and Human Service's Office on Women's Health, 2000; EDC, 2006). Dittrich (2004) stresses that of all the psychiatric disorders, eating disorders (especially anorexia) have the highest mortality rate.

Medical researchers Birmingham, Su, Hlynsky, Goldner, and Gao's (2005) study supports Dittrich's findings. The researchers studied 954 hospitalized eating disorder patients during a 20-year period; results showed "a high morality rate within the AN population" (p. 143). Their conclusions are representative of numerous body image studies that substantiate the statistics released by the U.S. Department of Health and Human Service's Office on Women's Health (2000) that conclude, "Eating disorders are one of the key health issues facing young women" (p. 1). This agency also notes that the mass media influence women's perceptions of the standard for the ideal, female body image and promote emotions of body dissatisfaction that are realized when these images cannot be attained. Therefore, the development of eating disorder symptoms poses a potential threat to the academic advancement and success of undergraduate women.

Purpose of the Study

The literature suggests a trend exists in the publication of increasingly thinner female body images in women's magazines. The purpose of this study was to investigate this perceived trend by using a content analysis to ascertain how undergraduate female coders would rank the female body images published in women's fashion, health, and fashion and health-related magazines viewed most often by female undergraduate students as listed by the Simmons Market Research Bureau (2003).

Theoretical Framework

Social Cognitive Theory

The research questions and hypotheses were explored in terms of Bandura's (1986) social cognitive theoretical framework. This theory, which focuses on observational learning, provided the theoretical basis for not only the determination of the research questions and hypotheses but also the identification of what data would be collected and the implementation of the data analysis. The social cognitive theory also served as a framework for the determination of what the researcher would consider to be knowledge.

Bandura's (1986) social cognitive theory posits there are three interrelated factors that influence human behavior: personal, behavioral, and environmental. These three determinates play a role in how people perceive reality.

This theory suggests that perceptions of reality are dependent on what people have learned through their own experiences or through vicarious observations of the behaviors of others. In order for these experiences and observations to have a motivational affect on the observer, the observer must be consciously aware of the modeled action and the consequences that can be expected if they model that action. Furthermore, the observer must internalize and retain the modeled action as well as attempt to personally replicate the model's behavior. Motivation to continue the specific behavior is based on the positive or negative consequences that the observer experiences after they replicate the modeled action (Bandura, 1986). Consequently, the thin female social models who are depicted as socially successful in women's magazines may be internalized by some women as the standard for femininity. Furthermore, this information may be retained as the

7

ideal, female body standard that will bring positive societal outcomes; therefore, some women are motivated to imitate these thin social models to attain the perceived positive social results.

Based on Bandura's (1986) theory and the literature, thin female body images in women's magazines may be perceived as role models by women. These thin female body images are often depicted as being recipients of positive societal outcomes (Garner & Garfinkel, 1997). The social cognitive theory explains why some women desire to emulate the observed positive outcomes that serve as a stimulus for pursuing patterns of behavior that appear to facilitate societal success (Bandura, 1997). Women observe thin female body images and internalize them as the societal standard for feminine achievement; therefore, these media images may have an influence on some women's future behaviors.

According to Silverstein et al. (1986), magazines contain large quantities of thin models who are portrayed as attractive and competent by the fashions they are modeling and the settings in which they are photographed. Silverstein et al. maintain that the social cognitive theory emphasizes that the more attractive an individual finds a social model, the more the individual will try to imitate the model. Furthermore, research conducted in the social learning field by Reeves and Greenberg (1977) illustrates that people are more likely to engage in behaviors that will help them replicate the lifestyles of admired media role models.

Therefore, Bandura's (1997) social cognitive theory and the literature support the exploration of the content of women's magazine media because research shows undergraduate women may be motivated to pursue unhealthy behaviors in order to achieve unrealistic body standards presented by the media. Since the perceived outcomes of the imitation of the social models presented in women's magazines may motivate women to pursue disordered eating behaviors to increase their self-worth (Forbes, Adams-Curtis, Rade, & Jaberg, 2001), it is important to discover trends and patterns in the sizes of the body images published in these magazines. A content analysis was used to attempt to determine the trends and patterns in body size rankings of the media representations of female body images in women's magazines for the years 1950, 1995, 2000, and 2005.

Research questions one and two were designed to ascertain what percentage of female body images in women's magazines were thin and which magazine titles had the smallest mean scale rankings of female body images in the 12 women's magazines during 2005. Research question three ascertained what percentages of the media role models for women were thin for the 36 magazines over the past 10 years. Furthermore, three predictions were created stating there would be no significant differences in the coders' rankings of the female body images between the years of 2000 and 2005, 1995 and 2005, and 1950 and 2005.

Research Questions and Hypotheses

The research questions and hypotheses were explored by conducting a content analysis of the female body images that were sampled from women's magazines that were published in the years 1950, 1995, 2000, and 2005. The women's magazines used to sample the female body images for 1995, 2000, and 2005 were the fashion, health, and fashion and health-related magazines viewed most often by female undergraduate students as listed in Simmons Market Research Bureau (2003). (Some of the magazines were focused on fashion, some were focused on health, and some had a focus that included both fashion and health-related content.)

Research Questions

Research question one explored whether thin media images were the most common female body images represented in the June 2005 women's magazines. Thin would be defined as a ranking of 1, 2, 3, or 4 on the rating scale.

Research Question One:

What percentage of the female body images in the June 2005 women's magazines represented thin female body images?

Research question two established a numeric rank (from lowest to highest) for the women's magazines for 2005 to show the mean differences (if any) in the number of "thin," female body images that appeared in the June 2005 issues. "Thin" would be defined as a mean scale ranking of 1, 2, 3, or 4 on the rating scale.

Research Question Two:

On a scale of one to 12, in what order (from lowest to highest) do the women's magazines rank in the mean scale rankings of female body images during 2005?

Research question three explored whether there were any mean rank differences in the coder rankings of the female body images for 1995, 2000, and 2005. Coder rankings for all 12 magazines were evaluated over all three years.

Research Question Three:

What percentages of female body images were ranked a 1, 2, 3, or 4 in the 1995, 2000, and 2005 issues of the 12 women's magazines?

Hypotheses

The null hypotheses explored whether a change recurred in the representations of the female body images published in women's magazines during the past five, 10, and 55 years based on Thompson and Gray's (1995) Contour Drawing Rating Scale (CDRS). Therefore, female body images were compared in women's magazines between the years 1950 and 2005; 1995 and 2005; and 2000 and 2005.

9

Three Hypotheses

HO_1: There will be no significant difference in the media representations of the female body images in women's magazines between the years 2000 and 2005.

HO_2: There will be no significant difference in the media representations of the female body images in women's magazines between the years 1995 and 2005.

HO_3: There will be no significant difference in the media representations of the female body images in women's magazines between the years 1950 and 2005.

Methodology

The purpose of this content analysis research study was to ascertain the perceptions that five undergraduate female coders would have of the photographic content of women's magazines that, according to Simmons Market Research Bureau (2003), were viewed most often by female undergraduate students. Coder data were used to discover the range of rankings and to make comparisons of the body representations of female body images published in the June 2005 issues of the following women's magazines: *Allure, Cosmopolitan, Elle, Fitness, Glamour, Harpers, Health, InStyle, Self, Seventeen, Shape*, and *Vogue*. The archived 1995 and 2000 June issues of these magazines were also coded to provide comparative data. The female body images from magazines that were fashion, health, and fashion and health-related during May 1950 and June 1950 included issues of *Cosmopolitan, McCall's, Seventeen*, and *Woman's Home Companion* and the June 1950 issues of *Cosmopolitan, Seventeen*, and *Ladies Home Journal*. The 1950 magazines were coded to make comparisons of years (with 1995, 2000, and 2005 magazine images) – not for individual magazine comparisons. (Only the 1995, 2000, and 2005 magazines were used for individual magazine comparisons.)

Data collected in this research study were used to determine whether thin media images were the most common female body images represented in photographic advertisements and articles in the 2005 magazines viewed most often by female undergraduate students. Furthermore, the statistics provided information to consecutively order the women's magazines (from lowest to highest) by mean scale ranking of thin female body image representations that appeared in the June 2005 magazines. In addition, the data showed comparisons of the female body images represented in the magazines during the past five- 10- and 55-year spans. Finally, the data were used to determine whether women's magazines continued to publish thin female body images despite studies that link these images to negative emotional and physical health issues in women.

Significance

This research study explored the extent to which thin female body images continued to be used as the photographic representations presented as social models in women's magazines. Considering the empirical evidence that has established possible links among thin female media representations and body image, and body image and eating disorders, it was the goal of the researcher to discover what percentage of the June 1995, 2000, 2005 and the May and June 1950 women's magazines contained thin female body images. Comparisons of data were made among years (1950, 1995, 2000, and 2005) and magazines (1995, 2000, and 2005) to determine any patterns or trends in the publication of thin female body images.

Organization of the Study

The implications of the social cognitive theory on this study have been determined by examining the relationship among the elements of mass media's influence on female body image and its links to body image dissatisfaction and the development of eating disorder symptomatology in women. Considering the negative physical and emotional behaviors and symptoms that are associated with eating disorders and the number of undergraduate women who are potentially at risk of developing eating disorders, this study adds valuable information to the fields of knowledge relevant to female body image representations that are prevalent in women's magazines.

This study also ascertains not only which magazines published the largest number of thin female body images for the year 2005 but also for the years of 1995 and 2000. Furthermore, the data provide information that shows there have been significant differences in the media's representations of the female body images over the last 45 years.

CHAPTER II

REVIEW OF LITERATURE

Introduction

The literature suggests that women in Western cultures desire to achieve slender body sizes (Forbes et al., 2001). Forbes et al. suggest that cultural messages are being communicated to women that support a slender standard for the ideal, female body shape. To evaluate whether women are responding to this cultural emphasis on a slender female body shape as the societal standard for body sizes in women, the researchers used the Personal Attributes Questionnaire to explore body dissatisfaction in 589 college students. Their findings support numerous studies that suggest society perpetuates and encourages women to attain thin bodies. Furthermore, cultural messages impact perceptions of body dissatisfaction in college-aged women (Forbes et al., 2001).

Dittrich (2004) posits that the internalization of cultural messages that glamorize thin female body images cultivates an increase in weight concerns in women. The American Association of University Women (1991) reports that the cultural focus on a thin female body image as the societal standard for women prompts girls to view physical appearance as a vital element in cultivating their positive self-esteem.

Body Image

Bierma (2003) defines body image as a person's subjective perception of how they think they appear to other people. In other words, it is how an individual perceives his or her physical attributes when he or she looks in the mirror. The Education Training Research Associates Resource Center for Adolescent Pregnancy Prevention (2001) defines body image "as the mental representation of your physical self at any given point in time" (p. 1). This includes his or her perceptions of his or her own body and how the individual thinks his or her physical appearance is being evaluated by other people (2001).

According to Bierma (2003), development of body image is a lifetime process. The experiences that we have and the feedback that we receive about our bodies from other members of society influence the way we perceive our bodies. Bierma notes that experiences and emotions we receive as children and adolescents about our appearance have a significant impact on the formation of our body images. Sheehan (2004) in her book, *Controversies in Contemporary Advertising*, concurs that the standards for beauty are derived from shared cultures and societal norms.

According to researchers Garner et al. (1980), since 1959 the societal standard for the ideal, female body image has increasingly promoted thinness. Dittrich (2004) notes that young women are under cultural pressure to conform to this thin ideal. The obsession with thinness has generated the need in some women to achieve body weights and sizes that are detrimental to their health (Garner, Garfinkel, et al, 1980.).

12

Garner, Garfinkel, et al. (1980) noted that by the 1980s, a trend had been established that depicted feminine beauty as being an ultra-thin ideal image. It has become the widespread consensus that eating disorders are a result of sociocultural factors and that the mass media are contributing to the social pressure for women to achieve extreme slenderness (1980).

Myers and Biocca's (1992) findings show that in the 1980s, the societal standard for the ideal female body size was becoming thinner; however, at the same time, women had begun overestimating their perceptions of their own body sizes. Therefore, the researchers studied 76 sorority women's perceptions of their body image after they had been exposed to television programming and advertising. This allowed the researchers to establish whether the media can have an effect on women's perceptions of their body sizes. They concluded, "Body shape perception can be changed by watching less than 30 minutes of television" (p. 126).

Furthermore, Mazur (1986), in his journal article, "U. S. Trends in Feminine Beauty and Overadaptation," noted that in the 1980s physical attractiveness had become important to the social success of women; therefore, women felt pressure to achieve a thin, ideal body size. Mazur's content analysis investigated the advertisements and articles focused on body shape and size that were published in popular men's and women's magazines in 1980. Mazur's findings suggest that women in Western society are increasingly subjected to cultural pressure to maintain a slender and shapely body.

Mazur (1986) and Sheehan (2004) note that culture plays an important role in determining the standards for the ideal female body image. According to Mazur's (1986) research conclusions, the cultural definition for ideal body image fluctuates. Mazur notes that societal standards for female body shapes have been changing from year-to-year, placing pressure on women to conform to these unpredictable and inconsistent beauty trends. In an attempt to adapt to the current standard of ideal body image, Mazur discovered that some women will strive to attain unrealistic, unhealthy body weights and shapes.

Turner et al. (1997) found that women would prefer to have a slender body and they are, at times, preoccupied with attaining a thin body size. These researchers studied 39 undergraduate women's responses to a body image satisfaction survey that was administered to participants after they had viewed fashion magazines. Turner et al. discovered that, after viewing the fashion magazines, the participants reported a desire to achieve unrealistic body sizes and weights represented by the thin models published in the magazines. Their research findings further suggest exposure to thin models can cause undergraduate women to exhibit an increase in negative self evaluations and body dissatisfaction.

Turner et al. (1997) findings suggest that perceptions of body image can be easily manipulated in undergraduate women. Their findings were supported by the research conclusions

13

of Wegner, Hartmann, and Geist (2000), who posit that college women's evaluations of their bodies are influenced by viewing images of thin models.

Szwarc (2003), R.N., B.S.N., C.C.D., in her size acceptance research series, Weighing Obesity, notes that in the United States the majority of the population in 2003 remains overweight; however, the nation has become preoccupied with becoming thin. Bierma's 2003 article in *Principle Health News* supports Szwarc's observations that the cultural cultivation of the unrealistic ideal body image is having a significant effect on some women's perceptions of the ideal body size in Western society.

Szwarc (2003) and Bierma (2003) report the need to achieve the ideal body image has been associated with a decrease in self-esteem, which can cause an increase in feelings of depression as well as other serious emotional and physical concerns. According to Szwarc (2003), "The obsession with thinness has not only affected how young people see themselves, but also how they view and treat others" (p. 2). Furthermore, Szwarc notes that the cultural pressures to conform to the ideal body standards represented in society are continuing to increase.

Nielson (2004) detailed in her newspaper report of a speech by Hawkins, PhD, who is the director of the Center for Change at Utah Valley State College, that the average U.S. woman is 5 ft 4 in tall, weighs 144 lbs, and wears a size 14 garment. However, she also reported that the average fashion model is 5 ft 10 in tall, weighs 110 lbs, and wears a size two garment.

Hawkins said that only "two percent of women in the world are genetically born to look like models" (as cited in Nielson, 2004, p. 1). She noted that 95 percent of the media depictions of women portrayed the ideal women as underweight.

According to Hawkins, these ultra-thin ideal representations of women have had, and are continuing to have, a serious effect on the U.S. female population (as cited in Nielson, 2004). At least 50 percent of 9-year-old and 80 percent of 10-year-old girls have become concerned about their weight (2004). Hawkins said that there have been children as young as 4 and 5 years old admitted to her clinic; these children have been participating in unhealthy weight control behaviors such as purging and vomiting (2004).

Hawkins relates that an estimated 90 percent of high school women are participating in personal weight loss programs (as cited in Nielson, 2004). Hawkins also reports that an estimated eight out of 10 of U.S. undergraduate women are involved in some form of disordered eating and 90 percent are regular dieters.

According to Myers and Biocca (1992), historically, research has discovered that body images can be altered by media consumption. Sheehan (2004) concurs that advertising influences the development of social roles and societal standards for the beauty ideal. Therefore, it is important to understand what relationship body image dissatisfaction has to eating disorder symptomatology.

Body Dissatisfaction and Eating Disorders

Body image continues to develop throughout a person's life and negative body images have been linked to the development of eating disorders (Bierma, 2003). Therefore, it is important to understand the relationship between body image dissatisfaction and eating disorders.

The Educational Training Research Associates (2001) Web site notes that body image is influenced by self-esteem more than physical attractiveness. Therefore, it is beneficial to understand what elements of body image affect women's self-esteem and how these elements perpetuate eating disorders in some women.

According to Bennett (2003), in Western society, instances of women experiencing negative body images are common; furthermore, the negative consequences of sustaining the cultural standard of a thin female body image have been emotionally and physically damaging to women in our society. Harrison's 2001 article notes that the perpetuation of the thin ideal body image can lead to body dissatisfaction and body dissatisfaction can encourage women to pursue thinness. This drive for thinness has been closely tied to eating disorder symptomatology, and Harrison's results suggest there is a relationship between decreased body satisfaction and the development of eating disorders.

In an earlier study, Mazur (1986) posits that cultural perceptions of feminine beauty are continually changing and that the increase in women's obsessions with ultra-thin models has prompted dietary abuses that are most prevalent among young women. Mazur notes that "many women diet to reach this slender ideal, some over adapt, starving themselves without realizing that they have passed beyond that point of optimal beauty" (p.281).

Bierma (2003) posits that the origins of body image dissatisfaction were developed through examination of psychological theories. This researcher found that women are bombarded with societal messages that promote feminine beauty as being physically underweight. Bierma posits that in order for women to develop a good perception of their body images, they must attain the ultra-thin body that is being transmitted as the appropriate standard for women. Bierma further notes that most women never achieve this physical ideal and they develop body dissatisfaction.

Harrison (1997) notes, "The two main eating disorders associated with the attainment of thinness are anorexia nervosa and bulimia nervosa" (p. 2). According to Mazur (1986), "The words 'anorexia and bulimia,' barely known a decade ago, are now in common use to describe self-destructive eating habits, particularly of young women" (p.1). Harrison (1997) relates that women suffering from anorexia have a fear of gaining weight and they refuse to eat enough to maintain a healthy body weight. Harrison also notes that with bulimia nervosa, women develop a

15

pattern of consuming large quantities of food and then vomiting, using laxatives, over exercising, or dieting to compensate for the excessive consumption of extra calories.

Forbes et al. (2001) study explores body dissatisfaction in European and U.S. college students. Their study suggests that undergraduate women exhibit more body dissatisfaction than undergraduate men. Furthermore, their findings suggest many college women are susceptible to the cultural misperception that the ultra-thin body image is an attainable body type.

Forbes et al. (2001) also suggest that the development of body dissatisfaction in college women can lead to dieting and eating disorder symptomatology. In Nielson's article, Hawkins (as cited in Nielson, 2004) relates that diets that continue to escalate could develop into dangerous eating disorders. In addition, Dittrich's (2004) Web site notes that deaths from the psychiatric disorder anorexia nervosa are the highest of any psychiatric disorder. The U.S. Department of Health and Human Service's Office on Women's Health (2000) further relates that eating disorders are chronic illnesses and the "death rates are among the highest for any mental illness" (p. 1). This government agency also notes that "eating disorders are one of the key health issues facing young women" (p. 1).

Given the link between body dissatisfaction and disordered eating, it is important to evaluate the major determining factor that promotes body dissatisfaction - the media. Dittrich (2004) notes that the majority of women have negative body images; therefore, viewing thin female body images in the media can further cultivate body dissatisfaction and eating disorder symptomatology in some women.

Media Influence on Body Image Dissatisfaction and Eating Disorders

Researchers Harrison and Cantor (1997) note that eating disorders are threatening "the physical and mental health" of many college-age women (p. 1). These researchers suggest that, for women, media consumption can influence and predict attitudes toward body image and eating disorders. Harrison (1997) relates that "the media play a significant role in transmitting thinness-oriented norms and values to children, adolescents, and young adults" (p. 2).

Harrison (1997) also notes that, "Historical trends and effects studies substantiate the claim that media images of thinness foster and reinforce a social climate in which thinness is considered essential to beauty, especially for women" (p.2). Furthermore, Sheehan (2004) states that when an advertisement stresses beauty as the criterion for attaining cultural success, important aspects of an individual's talents and how they can contribute to society are devalued.

U.S. Department of Health and Human Service's Office on Women's Health (2000) note that these sociocultural ideals of success include media images that portray successful women in society as thin and that this association with achievement and personal power can cause women to connect thinness with beauty and success. U.S. Department of Health and Human Service's Office on Women's Health (2000) further states that "media influences such as TV, magazines, and movies reinforce the belief that women should be more concerned with their appearance than with their own ideas or achievements" (p. 6).

According to Botta (1999), assistant professor of communication at Cleveland State University, current literature on media effects supports a relationship among media images, the development of body image, and the internalization of the thin-ideal body type as the representative body type for adolescents. Researchers Polivy and Herman (2004), University of Toronto, affirm that the media play a significant role in developing cultural perceptions that support the preference for slender body types in females.

According to Mazur (1986), the increase in the power and scope of the mass media during the 20th century has created a set of uniform standards for beauty. Mazur notes that media have been especially influential in establishing thin fashion standards for Europe and the United States.

Harrison's (1997) study concludes that there is a growing prevalence of media representations of ultra-thin models and celebrities. She also suggests that young adults exhibit a natural attraction to these media images, and they internalize the body types of these media role models as social standards of the ideal female body. Harrison posits that the internalization of these unrealistic media ideals can lead to poor self-images and the development of eating disordered behaviors.

The article "Body Image & Advertising" (2000) notes that women consume media messages and perceive these messages to contain credible information and representations of society's standard of the ideal female body shape. Unfortunately, standards that the media are transmitting as the realistic goals for women to attain are ultra-thin (2000).

Szwarc's (2003) article, "Dying to be Thin," states that exposure to the unrealistic, ideal, ultra-thin body image, which is the prevalent female representational standard in the advertising industry, has a negative effect on impressionable girls. Szwarc posits that girls develop a fear of becoming overweight. She further notes that the media representations of thin female body images cause some women to experience body dissatisfaction because they feel they can never achieve the societal ideal.

The journal article by Turner et al. (1997) , "The Influence of Fashion Magazines on Body Image Satisfaction of College Women: An Exploratory Analysis," supports this conclusion. The results of this study show that the media play a cultural role of not only reflecting established social standards of body image but also shaping the acceptable standards of body image. In their study, the researchers divided their participants into two groups. The women in both groups were close to

17

the same height and weight. However, one group viewed thin female body images in magazines and the other group viewed news magazines.

Once the groups had been exposed to the magazines, the participants from both groups completed a body image satisfaction survey. Those women who were exposed to the magazines with thin female ideal body images expressed more desire to achieve a thinner body size and had more negative self-evaluations. The researchers found, "Exposure to fashion magazines was related to women's greater preoccupation with being thin, dissatisfaction with their bodies, frustration about weight, and fear about deviating from the thin standard" (p. 5).

Milkie's (1999) research utilizes in-depth interviews to evaluate what impact media images have on females. The researcher notes that although the girls perceive the ideal body images in the media as depicting unrealistic media representations, they still want to attain the slender body types that are featured in the media. Milkie discovered that unrealistic social observations are linked to the development of body dissatisfaction, to an increased desire to be thin, and to eating disorder symptomatology.

According to Dittrich (2004), "The media promotes and reflects the current mainstream culture's standards for body shape or size and importance of beauty" (p. 1). Dittrich notes that when women are repeatedly exposed to media images of the thin-ideal body type, it can produce body dissatisfaction and increase a woman's focus on weight. She emphasizes that many women internalize media ideals of the thin body image and perceive these body images as real and attainable.

According to Body Image and Advertising (2000), current research suggests that media images have a negative influence on women's perceptions of their bodies. This Web site also suggests that body dissatisfaction can lead to disordered eating when women strive to attain unrealistic, thin body images represented in the media.

Dittrich (2004) has found that U.S. women strive to be thin because the media links thinness to societal symbols of success. In the media, "prestige, happiness, love and success" are represented as positive consequences of being thin (p.1).

Researchers Stice, Schupak-Neuberg, Shaw, and Stein (1994) have discovered there is a direct relationship among women's media consumption and their development of body dissatisfaction and their increased risk of eating disorders. They note that the more exposure women have to thin media representations the more likely women are to develop body dissatisfaction that contributes to eating pathology.

The research conclusions of Pinhas, Toner, Ali, Garfinkel, and Stuckless (1999), Clarke Institute of Psychiatry at the University of Toronto, support these findings that exposure to thin fashion models in the media can lead to depression and symptoms of disordered eating in some women.

Pinhas et al. had 188 female university students "complete a series of questionnaires" (p. 244). Next, the women were separated into two groups. One group was shown slides of female models from fashion magazines before they completed the second series of questionnaires. (There was a one week lapse between the completion of the first series of questionnaires and the viewing [or not viewing] of the slides and the completion of the second set of questionnaires.) The questionnaires were completed twice by all participants to examine "the relationship between exposure to the visual image of the ideal of female beauty in western culture and mood, body dissatisfaction, disordered eating" (p. 224). The study showed that women exhibited feelings of anger and depression when they were exposed to media representations of thin female body images. The researchers suggest that these media images can have a harmful effect on some women by increasing negative mood states, which can lead to eating disorder symptomatology.

According to Levine and Smolak's (1997) media effects content analysis research, the media are regarded as the single strongest transmitters of unrealistic female body images. The mass media are also considered accountable for the high proportion of college women who are dissatisfied with their bodies. Levine and Smolak suggest that the sociocultural, media-portrayed images of the current "beauty ideal" contributes to body dissatisfaction and eating disorders among female college students.

According to Garner and Garfinkel (1997), for several decades, the media have portrayed the cultural ideal body image for women as being ultra-thin. The fashion, entertainment, and publishing industries provide role models who possess unrealistic body sizes and weights. The researchers note that these thin female role models do not represent society's actual female population. However, some women in Western societies are motivated by media representations to conform to this thin ideal.

Steven Thomsen (2002), associate professor of communication at Brigham Young University, relates in his study on "Health and Beauty Magazine Reading and Body Shape Concerns among a Group of College Women" there is a connection between body image dissatisfaction and media consumption, especially in magazines. Thomsen suggests that exposure to beauty and fashion magazines can heighten college-age women's concerns for thinness and can promote the belief that celebrities and models represent the cultural standard for female body shapes.

Influence of Magazines on Body Image Dissatisfaction and Eating Disorders

Bennett (2003) has researched the relationship between popular women's magazines and body image. Her findings support the literature that suggests that the internalization of thin-ideal body images in women's magazines can "influence body dissatisfaction and negative self-perceptions" in female undergraduate students (p. 3).

Researchers Silverstein et al. (1986) found that women's magazines contain large quantities of thin models who serve as role models for women in society. Conclusions from Harrison's 2001 study suggest that there is a relationship between women's mass media consumption of thin-ideal body images in magazines and the development of body dissatisfaction, the desire to achieve thinness, and the development of eating disorders. Consuming magazine media appeared to constitute more of a risk for the development of eating disorders than viewing television Silverstein et al. (1986).

According to Harrison (1997), the strongest link to the media and eating disorders exists between magazine consumption and body dissatisfaction. Milkie (1999) also discovered that, in both qualitative and quantitative studies, women reported that they compared themselves with the unrealistically thin models in fashion magazines. When women compared themselves to thin body images presented in the magazines, they reported a significant number of instances of body dissatisfaction (1999).

Durham's (1999) research found that women are critical of the ideal body images presented in women's magazines, consider the bodies of thin models to be unattainable, and would like to see more diverse and representative female body images displayed in magazines. However, Durham also discovered that the same female respondents continued to idealize the thin body images that were presented in the fashion magazines. The female respondents continued to express that they believed that the thin media models were the ideal standard for attaining body satisfaction. They also responded that although they knew the magazine representations of the ideal woman were unrealistic, they aspired to emulate the unrealistic body images presented in the popular women's magazines.

Abra Fortune Chernik (1995), in her eating disorders essay, "The Body Politic," which is based on her personal experiences with eating disorders, notes women's dissatisfaction with their bodies and the instances of disordered eating have shown a marked increase since the 1980s. The literature suggests that independent research studies have discovered that there is a possible relationship among magazine images of thinness, women's poor body images, and eating disorders (Harrison & Cantor, 1997).

In a content analysis study by Milkin, Wornian, and Chrisler (1999), media messages on the covers of magazines were considered by the researchers to be alarming. The researchers discovered that unrealistic media messages (promoting a better life through weight reduction) were highlighted

20

on the front covers of magazines. These messages were positioned next to article titles that linked them to slender body shapes and the social benefits of attaining slender body sizes.

Harrison's (1997) research conclusions question the appropriateness of publishing media personalities and thin fashion models in magazines targeted at young females. The researcher's findings show that these images send "a dangerous message" and present unrealistic role models to girls.

Thin Media Representations and Social Cognitive Theory

According to Silverstein et al. (1986), women's magazines contain media images that portray thin models and celebrities as being attractive and competent. Bandura's social cognitive theory would support the hypothesis that when societal symbols of behavior are presented to women that indicate certain physical attributes will elicit positive societal responses, women may pursue actions that would help them realize the modeled behavior. Silverstein et al. (1986) notes that the social learning theory (foundational theory of the social cognitive theory) posits that the more attractive an individual finds a "social agent," the more the individual will try to imitate the "agent."

Thomsen (2002) and Posavac, Posavac, and Posavac (1998) found that women observe and compare their bodies with the physical attributes of idealized female media images. The social cognitive theory (Bandura, 1986) would posit that the physical attributes of idealized female media images serve as symbols of vicarious stimulus that influence women's perceptions of reality.

Bandura (1986) relates that people continually observe the successes and failures of others to determine what societal behaviors represent preferred behavioral norms. Martin and Kennedy (1993) note that continuous exposure to media representations of physical attractiveness may have an effect on females' "self-perceptions of physical attractiveness" (p.528).

Harrison (1997) also bases her research on the social learning theory, which she posits provides a basis for explaining why some young women are susceptible to media representations of role models who exhibit thin-ideal body images. Harrison suggests that Bandura's social learning process of modeling provides one "explanation for how young women may come to believe in the thin ideal and become motivated to engage in extreme dieting behaviors to meet this ideal" (p. 3).

Summary

The literature substantiates the need for this research study that explores if thin female body images are the dominate media photographic representations of women in magazines that are viewed most often by female undergraduate students. This study also provides a statistical foundation for future studies by providing data, measured by Thompson and Gray's (1995) Contour Drawing Rating Scale (CDRS), regarding the most prevalent female body images that are represented in the magazines viewed most often by female undergraduate students.

CHAPTER III

METHODOLOGY

Research Problem

Media messages containing ultra-thin, female body images can contribute to the current cultural belief that the female contour should be thin. Dittrich (2004) notes that to achieve this thin societal standard, some women will participate in self-destructive behaviors. Therefore, data was collected in this content analysis to establish whether thin media images continue to be the most common female body images represented in the photographic content of women's magazines that are viewed most often by female undergraduate students. This study also determined if there is significant difference among the means of media representations among the years 1950, 1995, 2000, and 2005.

Research Questions

There were three research questions examined in this study:

Research Question One:

What percentage of the female body images in the June 2005 women's magazines represented thin female body images?

Research Question Two:

On a scale of 1 to 12, in what order (from lowest to highest) do the women's magazines rank in the mean scale rankings of female body images during 2005?

Research Question Three:

What percentages of female body images were ranked a 1, 2, 3, or 4 (on a scale of one to nine) in the 1995, 2000, and 2005 issues of the 12 women's magazines?

Hypotheses

Three null hypotheses were examined in this study:

HO₁: There will be no significant difference in the media representations of the female body images in women's magazines between the years 2000 and 2005.

HO₂: There will be no significant difference in the media representations of the female body images in women's magazines between the years 1995 and 2005.

HO₃: There will be no significant difference in the media representations of the female body images in women's magazines between the years 1950 and 2005.

Variables

The independent variable for research question one was the year with the specified value of 2005.

The dependent variable for research question one was the coders' rankings of the female body images represented in the photographs from the fashion, health, and fashion and health-related

22

magazines of June 2005 that were viewed most often by female undergraduate students as listed in Simmons Market Research Bureau (2003).

The independent variable for research question two was the individual June magazines in 2005 that were viewed most often by female undergraduate students as listed in Simmons Market Research Bureau (2003).

The dependent variable for research question two was the coders' rankings of the female body images represented in the fashion, health, and fashion and health-related magazines from June 2005 that were viewed most often by female undergraduate students as listed in Simmons Market Research Bureau (2003).

The independent variable for research question three was the individual magazines in 1995, 2000, and 2005 viewed most often by female undergraduate students as listed in Simmons Market Research Bureau (2003).

The dependent variable for research question three was the coders' rankings of the female body images represented in the fashion, health, and fashion and health-related magazines from June 1995, 2000, and 2005 that were viewed most often by female undergraduate students as listed in Simmons Market Research Bureau (2003).

The independent variable for null hypothesis one (HO_1) was the year with the specified values of 2000 and 2005 that were viewed most often by female undergraduate students as listed in Simmons Market Research Bureau (2003).

The dependent variable for null hypothesis one (HO_1) was the coders' rankings of the female body images represented in the fashion, health, and fashion and health-related magazines from June 2000 and 2005 that were viewed most often by female undergraduate students as listed in Simmons Market Research Bureau (2003).

The independent variable for null hypothesis two (HO_2) was the year with the specified values of 1995 and 2005 that were viewed most often by female undergraduate students as listed in Simmons Market Research Bureau (2003).

The dependent variable for null hypothesis two (HO_2) was the coders' rankings of the female body images represented in the photographs from the fashion, health, and fashion and health-related magazines from June 1995 and 2005 that were viewed most often by female undergraduate students as listed in Simmons Market Research Bureau (2003).

The independent variable for null hypothesis three (HO_3) was the year with the specified values of 1950 and 2005 that were viewed most often by female undergraduate students as listed in Simmons Market Research Bureau (2003).

The dependent variable for null hypothesis three (HO_3) was the coders' rankings of the female body images represented in the photographs from the fashion, health, and fashion and health-related magazines from June 1950 and 2005 that were viewed most often by female undergraduate students as listed in Simmons Market Research Bureau (2003).

Method

The methodology for this study included completing a magazine selection process, performing a content analysis of sample body images from the 43 women's magazines, and developing a content classification for the data to extrapolate patterns and trends for the individual magazine titles and years. As noted, the researcher used content analysis as the research method to gather data for this female body image research study.

The operationalization of this study required that a multi-stage sampling of the documents be performed. To meet the requirements for inclusion in this multi-stage procedure, the photographs of the female body images had to exhibit explicit and detailed specifications of the content to be analyzed. A systematic random sampling within documents was performed on those photographs that met the sampling criteria for the three previous stages of the multi-stage sampling process. (The document sampling process is described under the "Samples" "*Documents*" section.)

The study also required the use of human participants to facilitate the coding process. A convenience sampling procedure was used to recruit female undergraduate coders. (The convenience sampling process is described under the "Samples" "*Coders*" section.)

The research design included Thompson and Gray's (1995) Contour Drawing Rating Scale (CDRS), which was used to rank coders' perceptions of the female body images in the magazines viewed most often by female undergraduate students. Coders used the CDRS to evaluate the female body images in women's magazines to determine ranking comparisons for the 12 women's magazines over a period of 55 years. In addition, the Statistical Package for the Social Sciences (SPSS) data analysis software program was used to analyze statistical data to determine any patterns and trends among the 12 magazines and the years of 1950, 1995, 2000, and 2005.

Content Analysis

This study investigated media representations of female body images in women's magazines. Content analysis was the method chosen to compare the photographic representations of female body images in women's magazines for the years 1950, 1995, 2000, and 2005. According to Bereleson (1952), the content analysis method provides insight into media messages by providing "objective, systematic and quantitative description of the manifest content of communication" (p. 18). Krippendorff (2004) further notes that "content analysis is an *empirically grounded method*" that can provide the researcher with data about pictorial images (p. xiii).

Bereleson (1952) notes that the content analysis method can be used to describe cultural patterns, reveal the focus of pictorial representations, and describe communication trends. Riffe,

Lacy, and Fico (1998) note in their book, *Analyzing Media Messages,* that content analysis is a method that can be used for "drawing representative samples of content, training coders to use the category rules developed to measure or reflect differences in content, and measuring the reliability (agreement or stability over time) of coders in applying the rules" (p. 2).

Samples

Documents

For sampling validity to be established, the selected samples from the population of women's magazines had to provide an accurate representation of the attributes that were inherent in the population (Holsti, 1969). Performing accurate sampling procedures from a precisely defined population allowed the researcher to make generalizations from the sample population of women's magazines that had a major focus on fashion, health, and fashion and health-related content. (It should be noted that when comparing magazines to magazines, the same magazine titles were used. However, when comparing years to years, it was not necessary to compare exact magazine titles. Magazines used to compare the years of 1950, 1995, 2000, and 2005 had to meet the criteria of: magazines containing fashion, health, or fashion and health-related content.)

Holsti (1969) posits that many content analysis studies require a multistage sampling approach. Holsti further notes that the initial step in multistage sampling is to define the sources of communication or "the universe of relevant communication" (p. 29). For the individual magazine comparisons for 1995, 2000, and 2005, the "universe" would consist of the women's magazines that were listed in the Simmon's Market Research Bureau (2003) database as being viewed most often by undergraduate women. For comparison of years, the 1995, 2000, and 2005 "universe" would consist of women's magazines that were listed in the Simmons Market Research Bureau (2003) database as being viewed most often by undergraduate women; the 1950 "universe" would consist of *popular 1950 women's magazines* as defined by Pastpaper.com (May 17,2006).

Holsti (1969) describes the second step in multistage sampling within content analysis as identifying "sampling documents." Therefore, the number of documents (magazines) to be analyzed was further reduced to include as "sampling documents" the June 2005 issues of the fashion, health, and fashion and health-related magazines viewed most often by female undergraduate students. The 1995 and 2000 archived issues of these magazines were also selected as "sampling documents." In addition, the May 1950 and June 1950 magazines defined as examples (from the 1950 "universe") of fashion, health, and fashion and health-related magazines by Pastpaper.com [May 17, 2006]) were: for May - *Cosmopolitan, McCall's, Seventeen,* and *Woman's Home Companion* and, for June - *Cosmopolitan, Ladies Home Journal,* and *Seventeen.* These 1950s magazines were also included as "sampling documents" in this study.

The magazines were only collected for the months of May and June. These months were chosen because research by Guillen and Barr (1994) showed female media images represented in these months made coding easier. The coding was easier because females were wearing garments that contained less material and covered less skin; therefore, more of the females' physiques were exposed to the coders (1994).

The magazines listed as meeting the criteria to be included as "sampling documents" by having a major content focus of fashion, health, or fashion and health-related information were: *Allure, Cosmopolitan, Elle, Fitness, Glamour, Harpers, Health, InStyle, Self, Seventeen, Shape, Vogue,* and *YM.* (YM magazine fit the criteria; however, it was excluded from the study because it was not in print as of May 2005).

Once the "sampling documents" had been selected, the number of images was further reduced by "sampling within documents." In this study, "sampling within documents" involved two stages.

The first stage involved reducing the number of images by sampling photographs of the female body images published within the 12 magazines for the years 1995, 2000, and 2005 and the seven magazines for the year 1950. Therefore, to qualify for inclusion in the sample of photographs to be subject to a systematic random sampling procedure, the photographs had to show the bare skin of at least one half of the female model's body.

For this study, the researcher defined one half of the female model's body to be equal to the exposed skin of two arms, two legs, one arm and one leg, one arm and the midriff, or one leg and the midriff. The female body images (fitting the criteria) were removed from the magazines and placed in a folder corresponding with the "year" in which it appeared. A number from 0 to 12 was placed on a picture in the folders to denote from which magazine title the picture was pulled. All images in the 1950 folder were designated as 0. In the 1995, 2000, and 2005 folders, images were labeled 1-12 depending on the magazine from which they were pulled. The numbers were assigned as follows: 1 for *Allure*, 2 for *Cosmopolitan*, 3 for *Elle*, 4 for *Fitness*, 5 for *Glamour*, 6 for *Harpers*, 7 for *Health*, 8 for *InStyle*, 9 for *Self*, 10 for *Seventeen*, 11 for *Shape*, and 12 for *Vogue*. The numbers assigned to each magazine remained the same for the years 1950 (0), 1995 (1-12), 2000 (1-12), and 2005 (1-12). According to Krippendorff, these are "sampling units" and they provide "a basis for judging the statistical representativeness of the data" and are the units from which the "recording units" are derived (p. 103). (The pictures in the 1950 folder were not labeled using the numbers 1-12 [representing the 12 magazine titles] because the 1950 images [recording units] were only compared with images [recording units] for the years 1995, 2000, and 2005 - not with individual magazine titles.)

The second stage of sampling within documents required using systematic random sampling. Krippendorff (2004) notes that systematic sampling is a good technique to use to create distinct subpopulations within content analyses research performed on "regularly appearing publications" such as magazines (p. 115).

According to Krippendorff (2004) and Neuendorf (2002), when using this procedure the researcher must select every kth/xth unit and begin the sampling process at a random starting point. Therefore, every fifth female body image was selected from each magazine within the folders for coding. The compilation of female body images in the 1950 folder was treated as one magazine for the systematic random sampling procedure.

To find a random starting point, each page in each magazine in the four folders was numbered between 1 and x (total number of images varied per magazine). Small Post-it notes were used to affix the numbers to the individual, female body images in each magazine.

After the images had been numbered between 1 and x for each magazine in each folder, note cards were numbered to correspond with the numbers affixed to the images in the four folders. The note cards corresponding with the 1950 magazines were then placed in a hat. Next, the researcher selected a note card from the hat to determine the random starting point for selection of body images for the folder representing 1950. This procedure was repeated for each of the 12 magazines within the folders for the years 1995, 2000, and 2005. (If a magazine title had less than five sampling units, all the sampling units were used as recording units.)

Krippendorff (2004) and Holsti (1969) note that objects selected for coding represent the study's "recording units." Every fifth picture selected by systematic sampling was defined as a "recording unit." (A permanent marker was used to eliminate all magazine titles/names from all pages.)

These female body images (recording units) were removed from the magazines and placed into black folders (described later in the study). It was not possible to evaluate every fifth picture in some magazines since fewer than five pictures in the magazine qualified for the study. When the content of the magazine did not allow for the selection of every fifth picture, all of the sampling units of that magazine were coded that met the criteria.

Finally, every fifth body image selected was numbered with a white sticker containing two red numbers separated by a hyphen. The first number on all the pictures was the number of the magazine title from which the picture was taken. The second number was the number of the female body image (in consecutive order it was pulled using the systematic sampling). All of the body image pictures were placed in a black folder according to the year in which they were published. The female body images that were placed in the black folders were the "recording units." The coders compared these "recording units" (female body images) to the female contour drawings in

Thompson and Gray's (1995) CDRS. On pages where several body images appeared, the body images that were not designated for coding had a gray X marked across the entire body image with a permanent marker to show it had been eliminated from the study.

Coders

Five female undergraduate coders were recruited from the population of female undergraduate students at a mid-Western university. The coders ranged in age from 19 to 22. All the coders were Caucasian, U.S. citizens who reported having the following heights and weights: 5 ft. 9 in. and 160 lbs., 5 ft. 3 in. 125 lbs., 5 ft. 5 in. and 132 lbs., 5 ft. 6 in. and 160 lbs., and 5 ft. 3 in. and 125 lbs. The sampling procedure used to recruit the coders was a nonprobability sampling (convenience sampling). Creswell (2003) notes that convenience sampling allows the researcher to choose respondents based on their availability.

Coding

Coding Process

Holsti (1969) states, "coding is the process whereby raw data are systematically transformed and aggregated into units" (p. 94). In this study, the coding process required that the coders evaluate a female body image and relate that body image to a figure represented in Thompson and Gray's (1995) CDRS.

Therefore, using Krippendorff (2004) and Holsti's (1969) definition, recording was achieved when the coder interpreted the body size of the female body image and then transposed that observation into a numeric format. Based on the drawings in the Thompson and Gray's (1995) CDRS, to ensure consistency in coding, it was essential that the coders receive explicit, consistent, and well-defined rules and instructions for coding (Krippendorff, 2004).

Coder Training

Neuendorf (2002) relates that coder training is essential to achieving intercoder reliability. Without intercoder reliability, the researcher cannot claim that the study meets the statistical criteria for achieving reliability and validity (Krippendorff, 2004). Each coder was asked to complete the study in a small, quiet office independent of the other coders. The environment also remained constant to help ensure consistency among coders.

In this study, coder training was facilitated by providing the coders with written instructions that provided explicit details of the coding procedure. These written instructions were contained in a code book (Appendix A). In addition, the researcher provided 10 practice female body images and a practice code sheet to each participant. The code book stated that coders were allowed to begin the study at any time they felt comfortable with the coding procedure. (All coders believed they were ready to code the body images in the study after coding only one practice picture.)

28

Code Book

A code book, providing explicit instructions as to what was expected of each coder, related the materials that had been provided by the researcher for the coder's use. The code book was provided to ensure that the content of the media messages would be analyzed and measured consistently among coders. Per Krippendorff's (2004) direction, the researcher designed the code book to provide instructions regarding selection of the correct categories on the code form, the rules for choosing among the rating and response options, the identification and rating of the body images, and the numbering schemata for the body images in Thompson and Gray's (1995) CDRS.

Instrument

Thompson and Gray's (1995) Contour Drawing Rating Scale (CDRS) consists of nine male figure drawings that were not used for this study and nine female figure drawings that were used to rank the body shapes of the females appearing in the 43 magazines. The CDRS, which provides "detailed, front-view contour drawings," is a user-friendly measurement tool that is quick and easy to administer (p. 259). Each female body shape in the CDRS was assigned a number from one to nine. A body shape ranking of number one represented the thinnest figure. The female figure drawing sizes increased to the largest body shape, which was to be ranked by the coders as a number nine.

The researcher used the CDRS because there were gradual degrees of variation in the female contours that represented the body shapes from thin to obese. For this study, there was no need to utilize a scale that provided the same number of thin and obese representations (to equalize the number of overall body shapes available for selection); once a ranking of obese had been established, there was no need to ascertain the gradual degrees of variation in the levels of obesity, only thinness.

The rankings for the female body sizes of the drawings in the CDRS were established by the participants in Thompson and Gray's (1995) study. The 51 female undergraduate students ranked the contour drawings as to which drawings from thinnest to heaviest represented a female drawing as being anorexic or obese. The female contour drawings numbered from 1 to 4 were identified by subjects as being anorexic. The female contour drawings numbered from 7 to 9 were identified by subjects as being obese. The female contour drawings ranked 5 and 6 were identified as being more average body sizes.

Thompson and Gray (1995) determined validity and reliability scores for the CDRS. To establish reliability, Thompson and Gray reported that 32 female participants (a subsample of the 51 participants used in the body image study) completed a self-rating test-retest to see if they could accurately choose their body size on the CDRS. (The test and retest were administered one week apart. The retest was administered after participation in the study.) Thompson and Gray (1995) note that a Pearson product-moment correlation of body size in relation to the CDRS figures revealed a reliability coefficient that was within the acceptable range, $r = .78$, and was highly significant at $p < .0005$.

According to Thompson and Gray (1995), "Validity of the drawings for assessing perceived body size" was also examined by evaluating the degree of correspondence that existed between the weight of the participants and their self rankings on the CDRS (p. 266). In addition, a final test-retest analysis of the correct successive sequencing of the contour drawings by the 51 female participants showed that 98.9 percent of the female and 98.7 percent of the male contour drawings were arranged correctly.

Procedure

After receiving Institutional Review Board (IRB) approval for the study, eight undergraduate females were approached (using the script that had been submitted to, and approved by, the IRB) to see if they would like to participate in the study. The undergraduate women had been nominated by professors and other female undergraduate students as women who might be interested in participating in this research study. My coder sampling procedure continued until five females were found who wanted to participate in the study. Eight female undergraduate students (two of which were minority students) were approached before the researcher found five who were interested in serving as coders. The five women who participated in this study were Caucasian undergraduate students ages 19 through 22.

The coders completed the study in a small, quiet office independent of the other coders. This was done to ensure coders' rankings were not influenced by the other coders.

Before beginning the study, coders were given the opportunity to sign a consent form, which included a list of their participation options. If a coder signed the consent form, the coder received: the code book (Appendix A); 10 "Practice" female body images and the "Practice Code Sheet"; 10 "Pre-test" female body images and the "Pre-test Code Sheet"; four folders containing the study's female body images, which were labeled 1950, 1995, 2000, and 2005, and the corresponding code sheets; and 10 "Post-test" female body images and the "Post-test Code Sheet." The coders' rankings of the female body images were coded on the code sheets.

Data Analysis

The computer software program used to analyze the data was the Statistical Package for the Social Sciences (SPSS). The alpha level was set at .05 for the Analysis of Variance (ANOVA) test, which was used to test the difference in the mean scale rankings for 1950, 1995, 2000, and 2005. The alpha level was set at .05 for the Scheffe test, which was used to test the difference in the mean scale rankings between 2000 and 2005, 1995 and 2005, and 1950 and 2005.

30

Neuendorf (2002) defines the procedure for establishing reliability as the process in "which a measuring procedure yields the same results on repeated trials" (p. 122). Neuendorf notes that for the data to be reliable it must be replicable.

The researcher followed Krippendorff's (2004) three basic requirements that researchers using content analysis should incorporate in the method design in order to use "observed agreement as a measure of reproducibility" to generate reliable data (p. 216). The first condition met by the researcher was to give the coders clear and explicit instructions for completing the coding assignment. The second requirement was met by selecting coders from a population with similar gender, race, and university admission requirement characteristics. (This would ensure it would be easy for future researchers to replicate the selection process for individual observers who would be used as coders.) The last requirement was established by providing a small, quiet office space for coders to complete the study that was independent of the other coders. The separation of coders ensured the coders' rankings would remain independent of the other coders' rankings.

Krippendorff (2004) posits that in content analysis "there are three types of reliability" that the researcher must take into consideration (p. 214). These three types of reliability are: stability, reproducibility, and accuracy. All three are dependent on the researcher achieving intercoder reliability.

Holsti's (1969) intercoder reliability assessment was used to establish intercoder reliability. This assessment was performed using the Program for Reliability Assessment with Multiple Coders (PRAM) software program.

There were 10 coded images in the "Pre-test" (used to establish intercoder reliability) and 10 coded images in the "Post-test" (used to establish intra-coder reliability). Holsti's (1969) reliability method showed that the coding procedure, which was repeated by five coders, yielded statistically similar results during repeated trials; this method showed an overall reliability coefficient of 0.94 in the "Pre-test" and of 0.92 in the "Post-test."

Lombard, Temple University; Snyder-Duch, Carlow College; and Bracken, Cleveland State University (2006), state on their Web site Practical Resources for Assessing and Reporting Intercoder Reliability in Content Analysis Research Projects that the researcher must choose "an appropriate minimum acceptable level of reliability for the index or indices to be used." Lombard et al. note "coefficients of .90 or greater are nearly always acceptable" (p. 4).

Stability

Krippendorff (2004) defines stability as "the degree to which a process is unchanging over time" (p. 215). In this study, stability (intra-rater reliability) was measured by having five coders use the same measuring instrument to code the same set of female body images in a "Pre-test" and a "Post-test." The "Pre-tests" and "Post-tests" were used to test the consistency of the coder observations and rankings and to ensure the measuring and coding procedures produced the same results for the five coders on repeated trials.

Reproducibility

Reproducibility is also known as intercoder reliability (Weber, 1990). Weber notes that reproducibility is evident when results from *"more than one coder"* provide similar coding responses. Holsti's (1969) method of evaluating intercoder reliability showed that, in this study, intercoder reliability was established for the "Pre-test" as 0.94 and the "Post-test" as 0.92.

Intercoder Reliability

To facilitate intercoder reliability, coders were trained to recognize and rate the female body images in the magazine folders, to use Thompson and Gray's (1995) CDRS, and to record their responses on the coding forms. Establishing intercoder reliability ensured that if other coders were added to the current study or the study was replicated by another researcher, the new coders would code the figures using the CDRS the same way.

Accuracy

To obtain accuracy, the data making procedure had to remain constant and conform to explicit specifications. Therefore, to promote accuracy, the coders and the "recording units" (female body images) were sampled using consistent rules and standards for selection. Furthermore, reliability and validity standards were established for Thompson and Gray's (1995) CDRS, and it remained the only instrument used for ranking the female body images. Intercoder reliability data was established using Holsti's (1969) intercoder assessment procedure. This procedure showed that the reliability requirement of accuracy was obtained for this study.

Validity

Holsti (1969) defines validity "as the extent to which an instrument is measuring what it is intended to measure" (p. 142). Neuendorf (2002) states validity in terms of, "Are we measuring what we want to measure?" (p. 112). Therefore, to establish validity the study's measuring procedure and reliability are import aspects to evaluate (Holsti, 1969).

Validity cannot be recognized without the establishment of intercoder reliability, which in this study verified that the coders could discriminate among the 1 through 9 contour body drawings and could successfully compare them with the female body images represented in the magazine photographs. Furthermore, as Holsti (1969) notes, validity also depends on the researcher's recruitment of coders who are representative of the population. In this study, the population from which coders were sampled was undergraduate women at a mid-Western university. However, the coders who participated were Caucasian; therefore, the representative population to be used for generalizations would be narrowed to Caucasian undergraduate women from a mid-Western university. This provided a sample of people with comparable characteristics, which included not only Caucasian, undergraduate, and female gender characteristics but also the completion of a diverse set of university admission requirements.

Content Validity

In this descriptive content analysis, content validity was used to support the validity of the conclusions that were derived from analyzing the collected data. According to Holsti (1969), content validity (face validity) has been the "most frequently relied upon," and is "normally sufficient" for, validation of the research when the method of data collection is based on descriptive content analysis (p. 143).

Krippendorff (2004) concurs that face validity is used most often in content analysis because it is based on common sense. Krippendorff notes that content validity is used more in content analysis because "content analysis is fundamentally concerned with the readings of texts, with what symbols mean, and with how images are seen, all of which are largely rooted in common sense, in the shared culture in which such interpretations are made, which is difficult to measure but often highly reliable at a particular time" (p. 314).

Internal Validity

To establish internal validity, the researcher created explicit and well-documented procedures that included the use of a consistent measuring instrument. Each coder followed the same procedure and used the same measuring instrument. Furthermore, participants who were recruited represented the population of Caucasian, female undergraduate students. These participants received a set of 10 pictures to code before and after the study to establish stability (intra-coder reliability) and reproducibility (inter-coder reliability). To ensure that the coders worked independently, each coder was placed in a small office independent of the other coders.

External Validity

To maintain external validity, the researcher used the data to describe only the manifest content that was investigated in this study. In my conclusions, the researcher did not make incorrect generalizations to groups, situations, settings, etc. outside the defined populations from which the media samples (female body images) were obtained and presented in the study.

Sampling Validity

Krippendorff (2004) notes that, "Evidence on sampling validity concerns the degree to which a sample of texts accurately represents the population of phenomena in whose place it is analyzed" (p. 319). For documents, a multistage sampling approach was utilized to ensure the female body images were an accurate representation of the entire population of female body images in women's fashion, health, and fashion and health-related magazines that were viewed most often by female undergraduate students.

To sample the coder population, a nonprobability sampling procedure was used. This convenience sampling procedure was appropriate for recruiting coders because the coders were used to evaluate and rank body images and not as subjects for manipulation. Furthermore, the coders that were recruited were Caucasian, female undergraduate students. These female students' perceptions would represent examples of the perceptions other Caucasian, female undergraduate women would have of the female body images sampled from the women's magazines.

CHAPTER IV
FINDINGS

The five coders were Caucasian, female undergraduate students between the ages of 19 and 22; they provided the body image rankings used in this quantitative content analysis research study. The coders ranked samples of the photographic images presented in the 12 women's magazines for June 2005 and in the archived 1995 and 2000 issues of these 12 magazines. Furthermore, coders ranked samples of the photographic images presented in seven 1950 magazines. It should be noted that the magazines coded in the study were not represented by the same number of pictures in the coding folders. It was not possible to evaluate every fifth picture in some of the magazines because there were fewer than five pictures in the magazines that qualified for the study. Therefore, when the content of a magazine did not allow for the selection of every fifth picture, the entire population of the magazine content that qualified for inclusion during the first three stages of the sampling process was coded.

The Statistical Package for the Social Sciences (SPSS) was used to obtain the tables and the statistical data necessary to evaluate the research findings. The findings are conveyed in a primarily descriptive format.

References to body size rankings was defined as: a designation of "thin" meant the body image was ranked by the coders as 1, 2, 3, or 4 on the Thompson and Gray's (1995) Contour Drawing Rating Scale, a designation of "average" meant the body image was ranked by the coders as 5 or 6 on the CDRS, and a designation of "obese" meant the body image was ranked by the coders as 7, 8, or 9 on the CDRS. Therefore, in this chapter, the patterns and relationships between, and among, years and magazines will be communicated based on the information that emerged from the CDRS and the SPSS data analysis program.

The answers to the research questions and the hypotheses were also investigated and described in terms of Albert Bandura's (1986) social cognitive theory. The social cognitive theory, which focuses on observational learning, provided the theoretical basis for the determination of the research questions, for the identification of what data would be collected, and for the implementation of the data analysis. The researcher labeled fashion magazines (F), health magazines (H), and fashion and health-related magazines (FH); these definitions were established through personal communication with a representative of pastpaper.com (May 17, 2006), which has been in magazine sales on a full time basis since 1998. The labels represent subjective opinions of the researcher and apply only to this study.

The first research question explored what percentage of female body images in the June 2005 women's magazines were ranked as thin by the coders. Table 1 shows the frequency scale rank percentages of the female body images for the 12 magazines during 2005.

Table 1

Frequency Scale Rank for the 12 Magazines for 2005 by all Coders (305 pictures)

Scale Rank	Frequency	Percent	Cumulative Percent
1	43	14.1	14.1
2	154	50.5	64.6
3	94	30.8	95.4
4	12	3.9	99.3
5	2	.7	100.0
6	0	0	0
7	0	0	0
8	0	0	0
9	0	0	0
Total	305		

This frequency Table 1 was used to evaluate what percentage of the photographic content of the 305 pictures from the June 2005 women's magazines represented thin female body images. The frequency table showed that the coders ranked 99.3 percent of the female body images in the 12 women's magazines for 2005 as "thin."

To explore the second research question, a numeric ranking (from lowest to highest [1 to 12]) was created using the mean rankings of the body images that appeared in the June 2005 magazines. The mean scale-ranking of each magazine was calculated by SPSS to determine the rank order of the magazines from 1 to 12.

Table 2

Table of Ordered Means for the 12 Magazines for 2005

Magazine ID	Magazine Name	Mean Scale Rank
9	Self - FH	1.87
1	Allure - F	2.00
8	InStyle - F	2.07
2	Cosmopolitan - F	2.12
11	Shape -H	2.19
5	Glamour - F	2.20
3	Elle - F	2.25
10	Seventeen - F	2.30
4	Fitness - H	2.42
7	Health - H	2.70
12	Vogue - F	2.80
6	Harpers - F	4.00
Overall mean scale ranking		2.27

F – Fashion   H – Health   FH – Fashion and Health

The Table of Ordered Means for the 12 Magazines for 2005 provided the mean scale rankings of female body images observed in the 12 magazines. A body image ranking of 1, 2, 3, and 4 denoted a thin female body image.

The 2005 women's magazines ranked lowest to highest according to their mean scale ranking of thin body images were: *Self* (magazine 9) with a mean of 1.87, *Allure* (magazine 1) with a mean of 2.00, *InStyle* (magazine 8) with a mean of 2.07, *Cosmopolitan* (magazine 2) with a mean of 2.12, *Shape* (magazine 11) with a mean of 2.19, *Glamour* (magazine 5) with a mean of 2.20, *Elle* (magazine 3) with a mean of 2.25, *Seventeen* (magazine 10) with a mean of 2.30, *Fitness* (magazine 4) with a mean of 2.42, *Health* (magazine 7) with a mean of 2.70, *Vogue* (magazine 12) with a mean of 2.80, and *Harpers* (magazine 6) with a mean of 4.0. Although the mean ranking of female body images in *Self* was the smallest and the mean ranking of female body images in *Harpers* was the largest, all of the mean rankings for all of the magazines fell in the thin range of 1 to 4 on Thompson and Gray's (1995) CDRS.

Table 2, the *Table of Ordered Means for the 12 Magazines for 2005*, indicates the differences in the mean scale rankings for female body images among the 305 body images in the 12 magazines during 2005. The chart depicts the majority of the means for the magazine scale rankings were plotted between 2.00 and 2.80. Only the mean scale rankings for *Self,* at 1.87, and *Harpers,* at 4.0, did not fall within the 2.00-2.80 range.

Research question three investigated any differences that existed in the coders' rankings of the 12 women's magazines for the years 1995, 2000, and 2005. Table 3, the *Summary of Thin Scale Rank Percentages for the 1995, the 2000, and 2005 Magazines*, showed the relative frequencies of scale rankings in percentages of body image sizes for the 12 magazines.

Table 3

Summary of Thin Scale Rank Percentages for 1995, 2000, and 2005 Magazines

Mag ID	Scale Rank				
	1	2	3	4	Total
Allure - F	23.3%	50%	26.7%	0%	100%
Cosmo - F	11.1%	42.2%	40%	6.7%	100%
Elle - F	21.5%	52.3%	26.2%	0%	100%
Fitness - H	5.6%	50.4%	36%	7.2%	99.2%
Glamour - F	22%	42%	30%	6%	100%
Harpers - F	15%	50%	20%	5%	90%
Health - H	8%	36%	44%	12%	100%
InStyle - F	13.8%	53.8%	26.2%	6.2%	100%
Self - FH	18.3%	45%	31.7%	3.3%	98.3%
Seventeen - F	13.3%	35.6%	33.3%	8.9%	91.2%
Shape - H	10%	45.9%	40%	4.1%	100%
Vogue - F	20%	35%	40%	5%	100%

For *Allure* (magazine 1), 100 percent of the body images were ranked by the coders as a 1, 2, or 3 (thin). The largest number of rankings of the body images for *Allure* were ranked as a size two, which was 50 percent of the magazine's sample photographs.

Statistics for *Cosmopolitan* (magazine 2) showed that 100 percent of the body images were ranked by the coders as a 1, 2, 3, or 4 (thin). The largest number of the body images in

Cosmopolitan were ranked as a size two, which was 42.2 percent of the magazine's sample photographs.

Summary of scale rank percentages for 1995 through 2005 shows that *Elle* (magazine 3) had 100 percent of its body images ranked by the coders as a 1, 2, or 3 (thin). The largest number of the *Elle's* body images were ranked as a size two, which was 52.3 percent of the magazine's sample photographs.

Fitness (magazine 4) had 99.2 percent of its body image rankings fall in the 1 to 4 categories (thin). The largest number of the *Fitness* body images were ranked as a size two, which was 50.4 percent of the magazine's sample photographs.

For *Glamour* (magazine 5), 100 percent of the body images were ranked by the coders as a 1, 2, 3, or 4 (thin). The largest number of *Glamour's* body image rankings were ranked as a size two, which was 42 percent of the magazine's sample photographs.

Statistics for *Harpers* (magazine 6) showed that 90 percent of the female body images were ranked by the coders as a 1, 2, 3, or 4 (thin). The largest number of body images in *Harpers* were ranked as a size two, which was 50 percent of the magazine's sample photographs.

An examination of the percentages for *Health* (magazine 7) showed that 100 percent of the female body images were ranked by the coders as a 1, 2, 3, or 4 (thin). The largest number of *Health's* body images were ranked as a size three, which was 44 percent of the magazine's sample photographs.

For *InStyle* (magazine 8), 100 percent of the female body images were ranked by the coders as a 1, 2, 3, or 4 (thin). The largest number of *InStyle's* rankings of body images were ranked as a size two, which was 53.8 percent of the magazine's sample photographs.

Self (magazine 9) percentages showed 98.3 percent of the female body images were ranked by the coders as a 1, 2, 3, or 4 (thin). The largest number of *Self's* body image rankings were ranked as a size two, which was 45 percent of the magazine's sample photographs.

Statistics for *Seventeen* (magazine 10) showed that 91.2 percent of the female body images were ranked by the coders as a 1, 2, 3, or 4 (thin). The largest number of *Seventeen's* body images were ranked as a size two, which was 35.6 percent of the magazine's photographs.

An examination of the percentages for *Shape* (magazine 11) showed that 100 percent of the female body images were ranked by the coders as a 1, 2, 3, or 4 (thin). The largest number of *Shape's* body images were ranked as a size two, which was 45.9 percent of the magazine's photographs.

Vogue (magazine 12) percentages showed 100 percent of the female body images were ranked by the coders as a 1, 2, 3, or 4 (thin). The largest number of body images in *Vogue* were ranked as a size three, which was 40 percent of the magazine's photographs.

The researcher also used Table 3, the *Summary of Thin Scale Rank Percentages for the 1995, the 2000, and 2005 Magazines*, to show that eight magazines had 100 percent of their female representations and four magazines had 90 percent of their female representations ranked as a 1 to 4. Furthermore, the largest number of body image rankings for 10 of the magazines fell in the two category with the other two magazines' rankings falling in the three category.

To explore HO_1, HO_2, and HO_3, Analysis of Variance and Scheffe post hoc methods were used to determine the mean scale ranking differences among years. The researcher first used the ANOVA test of mean differences to discover whether or not there were significant differences among the means of the media representations for the four years. The ANOVA test for 1950, 1995, 2000, and 2005 yielded an F value of 11.954 with a p value of $.00 < .05$. A Scheffe Multiple Comparison post hoc test was performed to discover which pairs of years showed significant differences. The results are provided in Table 4, the *Scheffe Multiple Comparison* table.

Table 4

Scheffe Multiple Comparison (all 43 magazines for all four years)

(I)Year/Mean	(J)Year/Mean	Mean Difference	Std. Error	Sig. (p)
1950/2.81	1995/2.51	.302*	.105	.041
2000/2.33		.480*	.101	.000
2005/2.27		.544*	.097	.000
1995/2.51	1950/2.81	-.302*	.105	.041
2000/2.33		.178	.083	.210
2005/2.27		.243*	.079	.024
2000/2.33	1950/2.81	-.480*	.101	.000
	1995/2.51	-.178	.083	.210
2005/2.27		.065	.074	.856
2005/2.27	1950/2.81	-.544*	.097	.000
	1995/2.51	-.243*	.079	.024
2000/2.33		-.065	.074	.856

Dependent Variable: Scale Rank   * The mean difference is
                                        significant at the .05 level.

To test HO_1, which compared the mean scale coder ranking differences between the years 2000 and 2005, the researcher had to explore if there had been a change in the representations of the

40

female body images over the last five years. The result of the Scheffe's test between body image rankings of 2000 and 2005 showed a p value of .856, which is larger than alpha that was set at $p < .05$ ($.856 > .05$). Therefore, this study failed to reject the null hypothesis (HO_1) indicating there was no significant difference between the coders' rankings of the representations of female body images between the years 2000 and 2005.

To test HO_2, which compared the mean scale coder ranking differences between the years 1995 and 2005, the researcher explored if there had been a change in the representations of the female body images over the past 10 years. To compare the 12 women's magazines for 1995 and 2005 as to the scale rank of body images, a comparison test using the Scheffe method was performed.

The Scheffe Multiple Comparison table shows that there was a significant difference between the 1995 and 2005 body image rankings. The body images became significantly thinner over this 10-year span. The significance between body image rankings of 1995 and 2005 yielded a p value of .024, which is smaller than alpha that was set at $p < .05$ ($.024 < .05$). Therefore, the null hypothesis (HO_2) was rejected because there was significant difference between the coders' rankings of the representations of female body images between the years 1995 and 2005.

HO_3 tested if there had been a change in female body images over the last 55 years in the 12 women's magazines. Scheffe's test between body image rankings of 1950 and 2005 showed a p value of .00, which is smaller than alpha that was set at .05 ($.00 < .05$). The Scheffe test showed that the female body images became significantly thinner over this 55-year span. Therefore, the null hypothesis (HO_3) was rejected because there was significant difference between the coders' rankings of the representations of female body images between the years 1950 and 2005.

CHAPTER V

CONCLUSION

The literature review describes the connections that appear to exist among undergraduate women's exposure to thin female body images presented in the media (especially magazine media) and women's development of body image dissatisfaction. The body dissatisfaction that is experienced when thin female social models are viewed in magazines can encourage physical and mental disorders in some women. Therefore, the literature substantiates the need for this study that explored the media trends in the publication of female body images in women's magazines for the years 1950, 1995, 2000, and 2005.

Chapter Five will communicate the purpose of the study; present a summary of the findings; and explore the societal, future and past research, and theoretical implications of this study. Chapter Five will also provide the research conclusions extrapolated from the analysis of the data collected using Thompson and Gray's (1995) Contour Drawing Rating Scale (CDRS).

Summary

This content analysis ascertained how five Caucasian, female undergraduate coders would rank the body sizes of female body images in women's magazines. These photographic images were samples of the female body images presented in the June 2005 magazines and the archived 1995 and 2000 issues of these magazines that were viewed most often by female undergraduate students. A sample of female body images in seven magazines from May and June 1950 were also evaluated in this research study. Data collected was used to make content comparisons among years and magazines.

At least 90 percent of the coders' rankings of the female body images published in women's magazines for the years 1995, 2000, and 2005 were ranked as thin female body images on Thompson and Gray's (1995) CDRS. Furthermore, the media representations of female body images became significantly thinner between 1950 and 2005 and between 1995 and 2005 based on the coder rankings using the CDRS.

The researcher discovered that thin female body images were the most common representations of the female body images in the June 2005 fashion, health, and fashion and health-related magazines. An SPSS frequency table showed that the coders ranked 99.3 percent of the 305 pictures as a 1, 2, 3, or 4 on Thompson and Gray's (1995) CDRS. (A ranking of 1, 2, 3, or 4 is considered to be a "thin" body image ranking.)

The largest percentage of coder rankings for the 2005 magazines was at a scale rank of two. The coders ranked 50.5 percent of the body images as a two on the Thompson and Gray's (1995)

CDRS, which was a coder ranking frequency of 154. A ranking of two represented the second to thinnest contour body image figure on the CDRS.

The second largest number of coder rankings for the 2005 magazines was a ranking of three. The coders ranked 30.8 percent of the rankings a three on the Thompson and Gray's (1995) CDRS, or a coder frequency of 94.

The data showed the third highest number of body image rankings was represented by only 14.1 percent of the magazine images, which was a Thompson and Gray's (1995) CDRS ranking of one. The study showed 43 of the coders' rankings in 2005 were considered to be a scale rank of one. A ranking of one represented the thinnest contour body image figure on the CDRS.

A body image ranking of four was noted as 3.9 percent with 12 rankings falling in this category. There were only two rankings of five, which constituted .7 percent of the coder rankings.

The mean of the coders' rankings for the 2005 magazines fell at the contour body size of 2.27. There were only two rankings that fell outside the "thin" body image range and both were a ranking of five. There were no body image rankings recorded that were above a ranking of five.

The researcher explored the percentages of thin female body images that were represented in the 12 magazines during 2005. The body image rankings that were 1, 2, 3, or 4 constituted a "thin" female body image. The women's magazines were ranked from lowest to highest in mean scale rankings of female body images published in the year 2005. These statistics were presented in the *Table of Ordered Means for the 12 magazines for 2005* (Table 2). The mean scale ranking of body images calculated for each of the 12 magazines presented from lowest to highest in mean rankings were: *Self, Allure, InStyle, Cosmopolitan, Shape, Glamour, Elle, Seventeen, Fitness, Health, Vogue*, and *Harpers*. The smallest mean coder ranking was *Self*. The magazine with the largest mean body image ranking was *Harpers*.

Table 3 provides the coder rankings of the differences among the 12 women's magazines' frequencies of rankings in percentages of body image sizes for the 12 magazines over a 10-year span. This table allowed the researcher to ascertain what percentage of the magazine images in the 12 magazines would be considered "thin" on Thompson and Gray's (1995) CDRS. To be considered "thin," the images would have to be ranked a 1, 2, 3, or 4 on the CDRS.

The scale rank percentages for *Allure, Cosmopolitan, Elle, Glamour, Health, InStyle, Shape*, and *Vogue* showed that 100 percent of the female body images in these magazines were ranked by the coders as a 1, 2, 3, or 4, which would be considered "thin" on Thompson and Gray's (1995) CDRS. *Fitness* had 99.2 percent of its coder rankings fall at a 1, 2, 3, or 4, *Self* had 98.3 percent of its coder rankings fall at a 1, 2, 3, or 4, *Seventeen* had 91.2 percent of its coder rankings fall at a 1, 2, 3, or 4, and *Harpers* had 90 percent of its coder rankings fall at a 1, 2, 3, or 4.

43

Harpers had the fewest coder rankings fall at a 1, 2, 3, or 4 at 90 percent. *Allure*, *Cosmopolitan, Elle, Glamour, Health, InStyle, Shape*, and *Vogue* had the most, 100 percent, of the coder rankings fall at a 1, 2, 3, or 4. However, all of the magazines had a 90 percent or above coder ranking of 1, 2, 3, or 4, which would be a "thin" body ranking according to Thompson and Gray's (1995) study.

Coder ranking comparisons were also made between years. Using the ANOVA test, the researcher discovered there were significant mean differences in the coder rankings over the 55-year span. Scheffe's test provided comparisons for the paired years of 2000 and 2005, 1995 and 2005, and 1950 and 2005. These comparisons showed there had been a significant change in the media representations of female body images during several different time spans.

Scheffe's test showed that between the years of 2000 and 2005 there had been no significant change in the size of the female body images that had been represented in the media. The comparison for 2000 and 2005 showed a significance of .856, which was larger than .05.

When comparing the mean differences of coder body image rankings for the years 1995 and 2005, the Scheffe's test showed that there was a significant difference in the media representations of female body images. The Scheffe's test showed a significance of .024, which is smaller than .05.

The Scheffe's test showed the largest significant difference in the mean coder rankings fell between the years of 1950 and 2005. The Scheffe test showed the significance between body image rankings between 1950 and 2005 was .00, which is smaller than .05.

Therefore, the study showed that there was no significant difference in the media representations of female body images that appeared in women's magazines between 2000 and 2005. Furthermore, there was a significant difference between the representations of female body images that appeared in the women's magazines between the years 1995 and 2005. In addition, the study showed there was a significant difference between the representations of female body images that appeared in women's magazines between the years 1950 and 2005.

These statistics show that the media representations of female body images for the years 1995, 2000, and 2005 were thin based on Thompson and Gray's (1995) CDRS. The statistics also show that the media representations of female body images became significantly thinner between 1950 and 2005 and between 1995 and 2005 based on the SPSS

Implications

The implications section will focus on the research, theoretical, and societal implications related to the present research findings as they apply to the study's contributions to the field of knowledge. The "research implications" section will include information on past and future research in the field of media representations of female body images in women's magazines. The "theoretical implications" section will focus on how the answers to the research questions and hypotheses relate to Bandura's (1986) social cognitive theory. Information in the "societal implications" section will include findings that pertain to the population of Caucasian female undergraduate students.

Research Implications

Implications for Past Research

This research study supports research findings that show media depictions of women have become increasingly thinner since the 1950s. Researchers such as Gagnard (1986) and Harrison (1997) support this conclusion that the media representations of models in women's magazines have become increasingly thinner.

Myers and Biocca's (1992) and Garner, Garfinkel, et al. (1980) established a societal trend toward a thinner standard for female body images in the media. This study confirms these researchers' findings, and the study's statistical data concur with information reported by Hawkins (as cited in Nielson, 2004) that the majority of media depictions of women portray the female body standard as being thin.

This study showed that the mean coder ranking of female body size in women's magazines for 1950 was 2.81, for 1995 was 2.51, for 2000 was 2.33, and for 2005 was 2.27. Therefore, this study confirmed past research conclusions that there has been a continued decline in the sample means for female body images depicted in women's magazines over the past 55 years. However, there was no significant difference between the population means for 2000 and 2005.

This study does not ask coders to rank women's body images in magazines using their personal judgments as the criteria for evaluating the size of the body image as thin, more average, or obese. For example, it does not replicate studies such as Gagnard's (1986) that require coders use their "own judgments in their evaluation" of the magazine images (p. R47).

As Mazur (1986) notes, cultural standards for female body image change from year-to-year; therefore, this study improves upon past research measurement designs of using coders' personal opinions for ranking body images. The current study defined a fixed standard that was used for comparing how the body images were evaluated for 1950, 1995, 2000, and 2005 by the coders. Considering the changes and variations in possible perceptions (definitions) of what constitutes a thin, average, or obese body size over different cultures, coders, genders, etc., using a coding instrument such as Thompson and Gray's (1995) CDRS makes replication results more reliable and valid. Using the CDRS helped the researcher establish consistency in body size rankings.

Establishing intercoder reliability was also consistent with past research; however, intercoder reliability tests for the majority of past body image studies might not be replicable for future studies. Although intercoder reliability was established for a particular date and population of coders, coders' personal opinions and evaluations could fluctuate over years, cultures, coders, etc.

45

Establishing intercoder reliability using a consistent coding instrument helped the researcher facilitate consistent intercoder reliability results that can be used for comparison with future body image studies.

The researcher found one study that used Thompson and Gray's (1995) CDRS in conjunction with other measurement instruments. However, in the current study, the measurement tool was limited to the CDRS because only the rankings of body contours, and not individual body features, were being coded.

Implications for Future Research

The Scale Rank for the 12 magazines for 2005 showed that 99.3 percent of female body images in women's magazines viewed most often by female undergraduate students represented thin female body images. Results of studies in Chapter Two present a possible correlation between the internalization of thin female body images and body image dissatisfaction in women. Furthermore, body dissatisfaction developed from viewing thin female body images in the media has been linked to the development of eating disorders in some women (Harrison & Cantor, 1997).

Although the literature suggests that the internalization of thin female body images in the media has an impact on body dissatisfaction and eating disorder symptomatology in women, thin female body images continue to be the predominate female body images in the 2005 women's magazines viewed most often by female undergraduate students. Furthermore, since the representations of female body images in women's magazines became significantly smaller between 1950 and 2005 and 1995 and 2005, it is hoped that this study will prompt further research into the intentions of advertisers and media that continue to present predominately thin female body images in women's magazines. The study also supports further research into media effects on women and girls when advertisers and the media publish thin female body images in women's magazines.

Although research shows that publishing thin female body images can have a negative emotional and physical effect on women, these images continued to be the most prevalent female body images in women's magazines during 2005. Therefore, studies might be initiated to determine possible preventative and rehabilitative measures within the medical and educational fields that could counteract the negative media effects of thin female body images on women.

This study should also be replicated with minority as well as male participants. All coders in this study were Caucasian females.

Theoretical Implications

Bandura's (1986) social cognitive theory provides the framework for why it is important to determine if thin female body images are the most common media representations of female body images in magazines viewed most often by female undergraduate women. Research by Silverstein et al. (1986), which is based on Bandura's theory, notes that women's magazines contain media

46

images that portray thin female models as being socially successful. These researchers note that Bandura's theory posits that people learn from observing the behaviors of others, and the more attractive an individual finds a "social agent" the more the individual will try to imitate the "agent."

The social cognitive theory posits that people may vicariously observe the actions of others and anticipate that if they imitate these actions they will receive the same positive or negative consequences (Bandura, 1986). The thin models in the media are perceived by people as realistic representations of the ideal body image (Botta, 1999).

Research presented in Chapter Two shows that thin female media images have been associated with negative emotional and physical behaviors in women. Many researchers suggest that thin female body images have been, and continue to be, the most common female body images published in women's magazines. Furthermore, much of the research presented suggests that the female body images are continuing to decrease in body size. This study provides empirical evidence, using Thompson and Gray's (1995) CDRS to show media images of female body sizes in magazines viewed most often by female undergraduate students are thin for the years 1995, 2000, and 2005. This study also reports that there has been a significant difference in the body sizes of the female body images published in women's magazines between the years of 1950 and 2005 and between the years of 1995 and 2005. In addition, the body images published in 1950 and 1995 were significantly thinner than the body images published in 2005. However, there was no significant difference in the female body images published between the years 2000 and 2005.

The social cognitive theory supports the relationship between the continued decrease in the size of the female body representations published in the media and the increase in the number of reported incidences of eating disorder symptomatology. Bandura's (1986) social cognitive theory also supports the conclusions that women observe the behaviors of the thin models in the media and internalize the perceived behaviors of these models as positive patterns of behavior. The thin models appear to be experiencing positive social results; therefore, the observers (women viewing magazines) may be motivated to strive to mimic these thin social models presented in the media. Therefore, Bandura's social cognitive theory supports the need for this content analysis that explored the media representations of female body sizes in women's magazines.

Societal Implications

According to Silverstein et al. (1986), magazine consumption is one of the risk factors that can contribute to the development of eating disorders. Harrison (1997) found there was a strong correlation between magazine consumption and eating disorders, which can lead to the development of body dissatisfaction.

According to the U.S. Department of Health and Human Service's Office on Women's Health (2000), one of the most serious chronic health concerns that is threatening the wellbeing of young women is eating disorders. Statistics show that deaths from the psychiatric disorder anorexia nervosa are the highest of any psychiatric disorder (Dittrich, 2004).

The cultural problem of eating disorder symptomatology has major implications for female undergraduate students. The continuing publication of thin female body images and the decrease in the body sizes of the female body images presents opportunities for further research into the long-term health issues, academic concerns, and personal problems that undergraduate women experience due to eating disorder symptomatology. Issues such as an eating disorder's effect on absenteeism, on grades, on financial assets of the students and their guardians, on emotional and physical resources, on the achievement of educational and personal goals, and on time management should be further evaluated.

Since Hawkins notes that eight out of 10 undergraduate women experience some form of disordered eating (as cited in Nielson, 2004), the implications of this study that show a continuation of the publication of thin female body images in women's magazines could constitute an issue of life and death for some undergraduate women. In fact, Harrison (1997) has questioned the appropriateness of publishing thin, female body images in magazines targeted at young women.

Another societal implication of this study is that it will make publishers and the public aware of where each magazine title ranks among the other magazines titles in the amount of thin female body images that are published in each of the 12 magazines. Not only does the study provide information regarding percentages and frequencies of thin female body images published in women's magazines for 2005, but also there is information that can be used by the individual publishers and the public to see how each magazine ranks next to other publishers' titles. This may prompt changes in some media messages within some magazine titles.

Limitations

The main limitation to this study was the gap in the magazine representations for 45 years. Due to time constraints, the magazine titles in five-year increments between the years 1950 and 1995 were not evaluated.

A second limitation was that Thompson and Gray's (1995) CDRS might be perceived by some as not showing enough body detail to effectively evaluate the female body images. Variations in breast and hip measurements are important elements for evaluation to some researchers; however, these body measurements were not evaluated independently of the CDRS. The limited number of body image figures, the CDRS only includes nine images, is also perceived as a limitation by some researchers.

An important social/cultural limitation was the lack of minority coders. Future studies should be performed with racially diverse female undergraduate participants as well as male participants.

48

There was also a concern that the coders might try to impose a research agenda on the study. The coders might rank the images larger or smaller depending on the how they perceived the researcher would like the data to be represented. This concern was based on questions that were posed to the researcher before coders began the study as to the intent of the researcher and the study. No research intents were provided to the coders by the researcher.

Also, since this was a content analysis, only manifest content was described. Latent messages were not evaluated.

Conclusion

According to Bierma (2003), the development of a person's body image is a lifelong process. Bierma also notes that the body image that a person develops is primarily based on how they perceive their physical attributes are evaluated by other people. The Education Training Research Associates Resource Center for Adolescent Pregnancy Prevention (2001) concurs that body image is not only how a person perceives their own physical appearance but also how they think their physical appearance is being perceived by others.

According to Sheehan (2004), there are societal standards that determine the cultural norm for feminine beauty. Garner et al. (1980) note that the idealized standard for feminine beauty that is considered to be culturally acceptable is the thin body image. The American Association of University Women Education Foundation (1991) concurs that the cultural focus is for women to maintain a thin female body type; furthermore, this organization notes that acquiring a slender body has become necessary for some young women to develop positive self-esteems.

Harris (1995) posits that there is evidence that links perceived body image with self-esteem in college women and that this link has an affect on their psychosocial development. However, the social information for the body standard that college women are using to develop their body images has been becoming increasingly thinner (Myers and Biocca, 1992; Gagnard, 1986).

Gagnard's (1986) study showed that the female body images presented in women's magazines during the 1980s were considerably thinner than those that were published in the 1940s and 1950s. Bierma (2003) notes that this continuous exposure to unrealistic, female body ideals in the media can lead to body image dissatisfaction. Bennett's (2003) study found evidence to support that viewing these idealized, thin body images in the media has produced body dissatisfaction in college women. Bierma (2003) relates that when women develop negative body images, they often experience symptoms of depression that can lead to unhealthy behaviors.

Body Image and Advertising (2000) Web site posits that it is the idealized female body images presented by the media that are cultivating body dissatisfaction in women. This Web site further notes that the media present standards of femininity that are unrealistic for most women to attain. The U.S. Department of Health and Human Service's Office on Women's Health (2000)

Web site concurs that the media provide social information that influences women's perceptions of the standard for the female body type. This agency further notes that the media promote emotions of body dissatisfaction that are realized when these images cannot be attained (2000).

Forbes et al. (2001) and Murray et al. (1996) communicate that these cultural and media messages of ideal, female body image are having a strong impact on college-aged women. Parham, Lennon, and Kolosi (2001) concur that educators should be aware that "up to half of any class of females will be suffering some level of problem" relating to eating disorders (p. 41).

Levine and Smolak (1997) posit that it is the media that are the single strongest transmitters of unrealistic female body images and that the mass media have typically been held responsible for the high proportion of college women who exhibit body dissatisfaction. Body Image and Advertising (2000) further relates that the mass media's perpetuation of an unattainable ideal body standard can lead to unhealthy eating behaviors in some young women.

This quantitative content analysis established that thin media images were the most common female body images represented in the photographic content of the June 2005 women's magazines viewed most often by female undergraduate students. The study further determined that the female body images presented in the media had continued to decrease in body size from May/June 1950 through June 1995.

This research study ascertained that thin female fashion models and celebrities continued to be the primary photographic representations published as role models in women's magazines during June 2005. However, Sheehan (2004) notes: "While the advertising industry avoids using models with larger body types in advertisements, evidence shows that consumers would welcome this imagery. The overwhelming majority of respondents to a Psychology Today study wanted models in magazines to represent the natural range of body shapes" (p. 112).

Considering that empirical evidence has established possible links among thin female media representations, body image dissatisfaction, and eating disorders in some women, publishers of women's magazines should reevaluate using thin female body images as the primary body images represented in women's magazines. Otherwise, the reported incidences of eating disorder symptomatology will, in all probability, remain constant or increase over the coming years.

50

REFERENCES

American Association of University Women Education Foundation. (1991). *Shortchanging Girls, Shortchanging America.* Washington, DC: American Association of University Women Educational Foundation Press.

Bandura, A. (1997). *Social learning theory.* New York: General Learning Press.

Bandura, A. (1986). *Social foundations of thought and action: A social cognitive theory.* Englewood Cliffs, NJ: Prentice Hall.

Bennett, C.L. (2003). *Effects of magazine advertisements on college females' drive for thinness, self-esteem, and body satisfaction.* pp.1-3. Retrieved March 8, 2005, from http://www.psu.edu/dept/medialab/research /Carrie.htm

Bereleson, B. (1952). *Content analysis in communication research.* New York: The Free Press.

Bierma, P. (2003). *Body image.* Principle Health News. Retrieved March 11, 2005, from http://www.principalhealthnews.com/topic/bodyimage; jsessionid=VUJPSIZZOYQSCTY

Birmingham, C. L., Su, J., Hlynsky, J. A., Goldner, E. M., & Gao, Min. (2005). The mortality rate from anorexia nervosa. *International Journal of Eating Disorders*, 38, 143-146.

Body Image & Advertising. (2000). pp. 1-5. Retrieved March 11, 2005, from http://www. mediascope.org/pubs/ibriefs/bia.htm

Botta, R. A. (1999). Television images and adolescent girls' body image disturbance. *Journal of Communication*, 49, 22-42.

Brumberg, J. J. (2000). *Fasting girls: The history of anorexia nervosa.* New York: Vintage Books.

Chernik, A. F. (1995). "The body politic," in listen up: Voices from the next feminist generation. Seattle, WA: Seal Press.

Creswell, J.W. (2003). *Research design.* Thousand Oaks, CA: Sage Publications.

Dittrich, L. (2004). *Above-Face facts on the media.* Retrieved March 11, 2005, from http: //www.about-face.org/r/facts/bi.shtml

Dixon, K., Kary, T., & Maccarone, D. (1999). *Body icon.* Retrieved September 25, 2006, from http: //www.jrn.columbia.edu/newmedia/projects/ masters/bodyimage/history/1960s.html

Durham, M. G. (1999). Girls, media, and the negotiation of sexuality: A study of race, class, and gender in adolescent peer groups. *Journalism and Mass Communication Quarterly*, 76, 193-216.

Education Training Research Associates. (2001). *Promoting Healthy Body Image.* Retrieved March 8, 2005, from http://www.etr.org/recapp/column/column 200111htm

Forbes, G. B., Adams-Curtis, L. E., Rade, B., & Jaberg, P. (2001). Body dissatisfaction in women and men: The role of gender-typing and self-esteem. *Sex Roles*, 44, 461-485.

Gagnard, A. (1986). From feast to famine: Depiction of ideal body type in magazine advertising. *Proceedings of the Conference of the American Academy of Advertising*, 41, 46-50.

Garner, D. M., & Garfinkel, P. E. (1997). *Handbook for treatment of eating disorders.* New York: Guilford Press.

Garner, D. M., Garfinkel, P. E., Schwartz, D., & Thompson, M. (1980). Cultural Expectations of thinness in women. Psychological Reports, 47, 483-491.

Guillen, E. O., & Barr, S. I. (1994). Nutrition, dieting, and fitness messages in a magazine for adolescent women, 1970-1990. *Journal of Adolescent Health*, 15, 464-472.

Harris, S. (1995). Body image attitudes and the psychosocial development of college Women. *Journal of Psychology*, 129, 315-330.

Harrison, K. (1997). Does interpersonal attraction to thin media personalities promote eating disorders? *Journal of Broadcasting & Electronic Media*, 41, 478-501

Harrison, K. (2001). Ourselves, our bodies: Thin-ideal media, self-discrepancies, and eating disorder symptomatology in adolescents. *Journal of Social and Clinical Psychology*, 20, 289-324.

Harrison, K., & Cantor, J. (1997) The relationship between media consumption and eating disorders. *Journal of Communication*, 47, 40-68.

Helser, L. (2004, January 14). Vanity sizing alive, well. *The Arizona Republic*, Retrieved September 25, 2006, from http://www.fitme.com/Fitme/html/ PublicRelations/coverage/ Vanity_Sizing_AZ_Rep_0104.htm

Holsti, O. R. (1969). *Content analysis for the social sciences and humanities.* Reading, MA: Addison-Wesley Publishing Company.

Krippendorff, K. (2004). *Content analysis: An introduction to its methodology.* Thousand Oaks, CA: Sage Publications.

Levine, M. P., & Smolak, L. (1997). Media as a context for the development of disordered eating. *The Developmental Psychopathology of Eating Disorders; Implications for Research, Prevention, and Treatment*, 23-257.

Lightstone, J. (2000). *Fat, thin, and power.* Psychotherapist.org. Retrieved September 26, 2006, from http://www.psychotherapist.org/ Index_archives_FatThinandPower.htm

Lombard, M., Snyder-Duch, J., & Bracken, C.C. (2006). *Practical resources for assessing and reporting intercoder reliability in content analysis research projects.* Retrieved July 12, 2006, from http://www.temple.edu/mmc/ reliability/

Marilyn Monroe.com. (2006). Retrieved November 7, 2006, from http://marilynmonroe. com/

Martin, M.C., & Kennedy, P. F. (1993). Advertising and social comparisons: Consequences for female preadolescents and adolescents. *Psychology & Marketing*, 10, 513-530.

Mazur, A. (1986). U. S. trends in feminine beauty and overadaptation. *Journal of Sex and Research*, 22, 281-303.

Milkie, M. A. (1999). Social comparisons, reflected appraisals, and mass media: The impact of pervasive beauty images on black and white girls' self-concepts. *Social Psychology Quarterly*, 62, 190-211.

Milkin, A. R., Wornian, K., & Chrisler, J. C. (1999). Women and weight: Gendered messages on magazine covers. *Sex Roles*, 40, 647-655.

Murray, Touyz, & Beumont. (1996). Awareness and perceived influence of body ideals in the media: A comparison of eating disorder patients and the general community. *Eating Disorders; The Journal of Treatment and Prevention*, 4, 33-46.

Myers, P. N., & Biocca, F. A. (1992). The elastic body image: The effect of television advertising and programming on body image distortions in young women. *Journal of Communication*, 42, 108-133.

National Eating Disorders Association. (2002). Retrieved January 31, 2004, from http://www.nationaleatingdisroders.org/p.asp?WebPage_ID=320&Profile_ID=41143

Neuendorf, K. A. (2002). *The content analysis guidebook*. Thousand Oaks, CA: Sage Publications, Inc.

Nielson, A. (2004). *Body image and the media*. NetXNews. Retrieved January 30, 2005, from http://www.netxnews.net/vnews/display.v/ART/2004/ 11/21/41a29c91199eb

Parham, E. S., Lennon, J., & Kolosi, M. (2001). Do all college students have eating disorders? *Healthy Weight Journal*, 15, 36-39, 41.

Pastpaper.com (personal communication, May 17, 2006)

Pinhas, L., Toner, B. B., Ali, A., Garfinkel, P.E., & Stuckless, N. (1999). The effects of the ideal of female beauty on mood and body satisfaction. *International Journal of Eating Disorders*, 25, 223-226.

Polivy, J., & Herman, C. P. (2004). Sociocultural idealization of thin female body shapes: An introduction to the special issue on body image and eating disorders. *Journal of Social and Clinical Psychology*, 23, 1-6.

Posavac, H. D., Posavac S. S., & Posavac, E. J. (1998). Exposure to media images of female attractiveness and concern with body weight among young women. *Sex Roles*, 38, 187-192.

Reeves, B., & Greenberg, B. S. (1977). Children's perceptions of television characters *Human Communication Research*, 3, 113-127.

Richardandkarencarpenter.com. (2006). Retrieved November 7, 2006, from http://www.
richardandkarencarpenter.com/biography-10.htm

Riffe, D., Lacy, S., and Fico, F.G. (1998). *Analyzing media messages*. Mahwah, NJ: Lawrence
Erlbaum Associates, Publishers.

Sheehan, K. (2004). *Controversies in contemporary advertising*. Thousand Oaks, CA: SAGE
Publications.

Silverstein, B., Perdue, L., Peterson, B., & Kelly, E. (1986). The role of the mass media in
promoting a thin standard of bodily attractiveness for women. *Sex Roles*, 14, 519-532.

Simmons Market Research Bureau. (2003). Simmons Choices 3 (Fall 2003) [Computer program].
New York: Simmons Market Research Bureau.

Stice, E., Schupak-Neuberg, E., Shaw, H. E., & Stein, R. I. (1994). Relation of media exposure to
eating disorder symptomatology: An examination of mediating mechanisms. *Journal of
Abnormal Psychology*, 103, 836-840.

Stice, E., & Shaw, H.E. (1994). Adverse effects of the media portrayed thin-ideal on women and
linkages to bulimic symptomatology. *Journal of Social and Clinical Psychology*, 13, 288-
308.

Stice, E., Spangler, D., & Agras, W.S. (2001). Exposure to media-portrayed thin-ideal images
adversely affects vulnerable girls: A longitudinal experiment. *Journal of Social and Clinical
Psychology*, 20, 270-289.

Szwarc, S. (2003). *Dying to be thin*. Tech Central Station. Retrieved March 11, 2005, from
http://www2.techcentralstation.com/1051/printer.jsp? CID=1051-072203E

Thompson, M. A., & Gray, J. J. (1995). Development and validation of a new body-image
assessment scale. *Journal of Personality Assessment*, 64, 258-269.

Thomsen, S. R. (2002). Health and beauty magazine reading and body shape concerns among a
group of college women. *Journalism and Mass Communication Quarterly*, 79, 988-1008.

Tiggemann, M. & Pickering, A. S. (1996). Role of television in adolescent women's body
dissatisfaction and drive for thinness. *International Journal of Eating Disorders*, 20, 199-
203.

Turner, S. L., Hamilton, H., Jacobs, M., Angood, L. M., & Dwyer, D. H. (1997). The influence of
fashion magazines o the body image satisfaction of college women: An exploratory analysis.
Adolescence, 32, 603-615.

U.S. Department of Health and Human Service's Office on Women's Health. (2000). *Information
Sheet February 2000 Eating Disorders*. Retrieved July 16, 2006, from http://www.
womenshealth.gov/owth/pub/factsheets/eatingdis.htm

Weber, R. P. (1990). *Basic content analysis* (2nd ed.). Newbury Park, CA: Sage.

Wegner, B. S., Hartmann, A. M., & Geist, C. R. (2000). Effect of exposure to photographs of thin models on self-consciousness in female college students. *Psychological Reports*, 86, 1149-1154.

Wiseman, C. V., Gray, J. J., Mosimann, J. E., & Ahrens, A. H. (1992). Cultural expectations of thinness in women: An update. *International Journal of Eating Disorders*, 11, 85-89.

APPENDIX A

CODE BOOK

(Please read all instructions in this code book before beginning the study.)

The code book provides instructions regarding selection of the correct categories on the code form, the rules for choosing among the ranking options, and the numbering schemata for the body images on the Thompson and Gray's (1995) Contour Body Rating Scale (CDRS).

You should have received the following items from the researcher in the order listed below:

1. consent form
2. code book
3. magnifying glass
4. sponge - to wet fingers
5. mechanical pencils
6. nine female figure drawings with the words "Thompson and Gray's 1995 CDRS" written on the back.
7. a folder labeled "Practice" containing female body images and a code sheet labeled "Practice Code Sheet."
8. a folder labeled "Pre-test" containing female body images and a code sheet labeled "Pre-test Code Sheet."
9. four folders labeled 1950, 1995, 2000, and 2005 (in that order) containing the "Test" body images for the study. Code the body images in these folders in the order of 1950, 1995, 2000, and 2005.
10. four pages (stapled) of code sheets that are labeled "Test Code Sheets" to rank the body images in the four folders labeled with years.
11. a folder labeled "Post-test" containing female body images and a code sheet labeled "Post-test Code Sheet.

Directions/steps to complete the study:

1. First, the researcher will record your age, height, weight, race, and university   enrollment status.
2. In the first folder, you will be coding practice body images onto a "Practice Code Sheet." (You may proceed to the next step [number 3], which is the next folder, as soon as you are comfortable with the coding process. You do not have to code all 10 practice pictures.)
   a. The practice body images are marked with a white sticker that has two red numbers separated by a hyphen on them. The first number on the pictures will be a 14. The second number will be a number from one to 10.

78

b. Ignore all body images marked with a gray X in all folders.

c. Your "Practice Code Sheet" columns will be labeled with the words: Year, Mag ID, Photo #, Scale Rank, and Coder #. (Please ignore the "Coder #" and "Year" columns on all code sheets.)

d. You will see a number 14 under the "Mag ID" column of your code sheet, which represents the first number (14) on the white sticker on each body image. You will see a number from 1 to 10 under the "Photo #"column of your code sheet, which represents the second number on the sticker on each body image. The numbers on the stickers that are on the body images will correspond with the numbers under the "Mag ID" and "Photo #" columns on your code sheet. For example, body image sticker representation 14-1 will correspond with the code sheet numbers 14-1, which are "Mag ID" 14 and "Photo #" 1 columns.

e. The "Scale Rank" column on the "Practice Code Sheet" is where you rank each body image marked with a white sticker and two red numbers as to what body size (1 to 9 ranking) it looks like on the CDRS. (The CDRS has nine women's body images drawn on it.)

The thinnest figure would be considered "figure one" and the largest figure would be considered "figure nine." (Feel free to write the numbers [1 through 9)] on the CDRS sheet beside/under the appropriate body figures.)

3. In the second folder, you will be coding "Pre-test" body images.

a. All body images are marked with a white sticker that has two red numbers on it. The first number will be a 13. The second number will be a number from one to 10.

b. On the "Pre-test Code Sheet," you will see a number 13 under the "Mag ID" column, which represents the first number on the white sticker on each body image. There will also be a number from one to 10 under the "Photo #" column that represents the second number on the sticker on each picture. For example, sticker 13-1 will correspond with code sheet columns "Mag ID" 13 and "Photo #" 1.

c. The "Pre-test Code Sheet" column labeled "Scale Rank" is where you rank the body size of the body image that has the corresponding white sticker number. Rank each body image marked with a white sticker and two red numbers as to what body size (1 to 9 ranking) it looks like on the CDRS sheet.

4. Next, you will be coding pictures from the four folders labeled 1950, 1995, 2000, and 2005. You will use the same coding procedure that you used in your "Practice" and "Pre-test" coding exercises above. You will rank the body sizes of the body images on the "Test Code Sheets."

5. Finally, in the last folder, you will be coding "Post-test" body images. You will write the
   rankings of the body images on code sheets labeled "Post-test."

VDM

Verlag
Dr. Müller

Wissenschaftlicher Buchverlag bietet

kostenfreie

Publikation

von

wissenschaftlichen Arbeiten

Diplomarbeiten, Magisterarbeiten, Master und Bachelor Theses
sowie Dissertationen, Habilitationen und wissenschaftliche Monographien

Sie verfügen über eine wissenschaftliche Abschlußarbeit zu aktuellen oder zeitlosen
Fragestellungen, die hohen inhaltlichen und formalen Ansprüchen genügt,
und haben **Interesse an einer honorarvergüteten Publikation**?

Dann senden Sie bitte erste Informationen über Ihre Arbeit per Email
an info@vdm-verlag.de. Unser Außenlektorat meldet sich umgehend bei Ihnen.

VDM Verlag Dr. Müller Aktiengesellschaft & Co. KG
Dudweiler Landstraße 125a
D - 66123 Saarbrücken

www.vdm-verlag.de

Printed in the United Kingdom by
Lightning Source UK Ltd., Milton Keynes
140218UK00001B/31/P